TWO GREAT SCOUTS

AND THEIR PAWNEE BATTALION

The Experiences of Frank J. North and Luther H. North, Pioneers in the Great West, 1856-1882, and their defence of the building of the Union Pacific Railroad by

GEORGE BIRD GRINNELL

1928

Contents

PUBLISHER'S NOTES

This is but one of the more obscure but fascinating books by the noted historian, naturalist, and anthropologist, George Bird Grinnell. In his many years of traveling and exploring the western frontier, Grinnell met everyone of note and wrote of many of them. A Yale graduate with a degree in zoology, he was an early conservationist and worked hard to prevent the extinction of the buffalo.

Grinnell was also the editor and publisher of *Forest and Stream* magazine, a popular and influential sportsmen's periodical. He often used his magazine to advocate for preservation of lands such as Yellowstone. Legislation in 1894, promoted by Grinnell, helped save the last wild herd of buffalo in Yellowstone and outlaw poaching and vandalism in the Park.

Grinnell was a major force in the creation of Glacier National Park. He was a friend of Theodore Roosevelt, who was a great admirer of Grinnell.

In this work, Grinnell turned his attention to two brothers of whom most Americans have never heard. Frank Joshua North was the older of the two brothers and went west in 1856 at the tender age of 16. While he was a teamster in the region, he met and befriended the Pawnees, learning to speak their language.

Luther was born in 1844 in Ohio and served in the Civil War, later joining his brother in the west.

INTRODUCTION

About the middle of the last century a large part of our country west of the Mississippi river was known as the Far West. It lay beyond areas reached by railroads and was quite unknown. Except for a few trading posts and military forts it was without white residents. Yet there were roads through it, the California and Oregon trail for emigrants and the Santa Fe trail, a commercial route to Mexico. Besides, it had been traversed in many directions by the trappers of the beaver-the first explorers of the west. Those who passed through it in search of fur, however, seldom set down the details of their journeyings, and up to the latter part of the nineteenth century much of the region was unexplored.

Transportation in that Far West was very different from the transportation of today. Other than on foot, there were two methods of travel on horseback or by wagon. Baggage and freight were carried in wagons hauled by oxen, mules or horses, where wheeled vehicles could be used. Individuals rode on horseback. This horseback riding was serious work. The journeys made by the traveler covered hundreds of miles and he was obliged to ride the same horse, day after day. This horse subsisted on the prairie grass picked up between the end of one day's ride and the beginning of the next day. To endure this continuous work, it was necessary that the horse be kept in good condition. For this reason, the pace was slow and the distances covered were not great. The gait was a walk and twenty or at most twenty-five miles was the usual length of the day's march about the rate of travel of a man on foot. Most horses walked from two and one half to three miles an hour. One that walked as fast as four miles an hour was unusual. Thus the traveler moved slowly and each journey between distant points took a long time. In military expeditions in the west many years ago, the infantry usually kept up well with the cavalry.

Through many regions of the Far West one might travel for weeks or months without seeing people or signs of civilized occupation. Wild animals buffalo, elk, deer, antelope and wolves-were often abundant. Men were seldom seen. If met with, they were likely to be hostile Indians and that meant either a race to escape them, or possibly a fight. The unexpected appearance of men on horseback always caused a feeling of doubt, until they had come near enough to be identified.

The occupancy by white people of portions of the western territory, followed soon after the expulsion of the Indians. That territory had been the feeding ground of the buffalo which were the Indian's support. The first whites who entered the country killed and drove off the buffalo. Other whites came, who wished to become permanent occupants of the soil and to use the old buffalo pastures for the cultivation of agricultural crops. Now that there were no longer buffalo, what had been the Indian hunting ground became his battle ground against the whites. Thus the people who occupied this region were chiefly hostile Indians. This was their country; it belonged to them and they objected to its invasion by the white people, who drove away the game, occupied the land and interfered with the Indian mode of life. Then too, since the white people possessed many things that the Indians wished to have, groups of young men were likely to try to capture such things for themselves. The white owners defended their property and this led to fighting. One fight was likely to bring about another and then followed wars.

In such Indian wars troops and other fighting men were called out and people were needed who were acquainted with the new country and with the ways of the enemy those who could guide the fighting men about and help them to get in close touch with their foes.

Some of the keenest scouts in the wars of the early west were Indians. Of the white scouts, the best equipped were those who knew most about the Indians. Having a better understanding of how Indians would reason and react under certain conditions, they were especially competent to conclude what the enemy would be likely to do.

The life of a scout was full of peril, yet because he was always ready and prepared for whatever might happen, he was constantly escaping dangers, overcoming difficult situations and reappearing, after it was feared that he had been lost. Yet battle, winter and accident often claimed the lives of these men. Most scouts were men

3

of high devotion to duty. Charlie Reynolds,* one of the greatest scouts of his day, gave his life in the effort to offer an opportunity to save themselves to the men of Reno's command. Almost his last words to the few civilian scouts with him, spoken while Reno's men were seeking safety by rushing toward the crossing of the river were: "Hold on, boys, let's try to stop these Indians while the soldiers get across." The charging Indians were too many and a moment later he fell.

*"Lonesome Charlie" Reynolds was one of the most famous scouts of his day and highly respected by all. A friend of his, testifying at the Reno Court of Inquiry in 1879, stated that Charlie had had a premonition of his death on the 1876 expedition. He asked to be relieved of duty but General Terry talked him into staying.—Ed. 2015

The North brothers had been residents of the frontier from boyhood and experience had taught them the ways of its wild inhabitants and methods of self dependence in unknown regions. More than that, they had long been in close contact with the Pawnee Indians, who then, and for years thereafter, preserved and practiced many of their old time ways of life. In those days the Pawnees still made war excursions against their tribal enemies and often returned with much plunder, of which horses, as the most valuable and easily taken property, were the chief prizes. With this training and with this association, the North brothers became great scouts, singularly fitted to take part in Indian warfare. The service they rendered during their fighting days cannot be too highly praised. Its value to the country was enormous.

These men were brave, as in the old war days most men were, because they thought of their work and not of themselves. Fear is based on the contemplation of self of some occurrence that one thinks may affect him adversely. Almost every act that we perform has in it possibilities of accident or danger, yet these possibilities are seldom considered. A small boy climbing a tree, a mountaineer making a difficult ascent, may each be in a situation of danger, but neither feels fear because neither thinks of the danger. The mind of each is fixed on his objective; each is thinking only of what he wishes to accomplish and how he may succeed. If, before starting to climb, each had contemplated the possibility of a fall and injury or death, perhaps neither would have climbed.

In these old fightings, the men who took part in them were not concerned about what might happen to themselves. They were thinking of defeating and driving off the enemy. That they themselves might be injured did not occur to them.

In their own view, the daily life of such men covered only the commonplace. They went on from day to day doing only what they had promised to do-fulfilling their agreements. The men of the present day cannot conceive of the risks and the labors involved in that old wild life. They have had no experience to make them understand this.

In the year 1864, hostile Indians were troublesome in the plains country especially in the valley of the Platte river. It was in this year that General S. R. Curtis, having seen something of Frank J. North and knowing of his association with the Pawnees, conceived the idea of engaging Pawnee scouts to work with the troops. Not very long after that Frank North was directed to go to the Pawnee agency and to enlist a number of Pawnee warriors to serve as scouts.

The survey of the Union Pacific railroad ran at no great distance from military posts where troops were stationed and these troops prevented some Indian depredations. But when Major North and his Pawnee scouts were stationed along the line of the railroad then building, they gave the hostiles a sharp check. The Pawnees, well-armed and well mounted, were always ready to attack and follow raiding parties, while it took time to summon the troops from any fort to the point of attack.

See Grenville Dodge's How We Built the Union Pacific Railway.*—Ed. 2015*

This promptness and activity soon spread among the hostile Indians the knowledge that an effective fighting force was scattered along the railroad and that they must use caution in their raids. Besides this the Pawnee scouts were frequently moved and appeared in unexpected places, and therefore the hostiles never knew where they might show themselves. The defense of the railroad by the

Pawnees thus presented to the hostile Indians an aspect very different from that offered by the white troops.

Major Frank North died in 1885, in his early middle life. He was a great leader of men and his character won for him the absolute devotion and trust of those he commanded. Whether it was by his good fortune or his skill, he never lost a man in battle. This no doubt was in part an explanation of the faith his men had in him—in his success. Himself always in the forefront of the battle, he never said to his men "Go on" but always "Come along" and his men always strove to keep up with him.

Needless to say, he was brave and he expected in his men the courage and steadfastness that he himself possessed. In one fight when he and his scouts were in the open, exposed to the fire of concealed enemies and some of his men showed a disposition to retreat, Frank North said to them, "I shall kill the first man that runs." No one ran.

The experiences of Captain L. H. North cover more years than those of his brother and so are wider. His journeyings have extended from the international boundary, south through Oklahoma (the old Indian Territory) and he has spent much time in the Rocky mountains. He is today the greatest, as he is almost the last, of the old-time scouts of America.

His knowledge of the Indian and of the Indian's ways of thought is profound. As a hunter of wild game he was most expert and successful and the most certain and best rifle shot that I have seen.

At this late day few men survive who were scouts in the Indian wars. Of these, Captain North is probably the oldest as he is certainly the most experienced and the most able. Captain North and his brother, Frank North, were in the class with Bridger and Carson. They, and such as they, did the tremendous work of making available what is sometimes called our western empire.

The development of the western country, its opening to settlement, and so its productivity, was accomplished in comparatively few years. During these years a multitude of important events took place that have never been recorded. Yet in

6

order that we may understand the history of those years, as many of these events as can be learned should be set down. One of the most useful steps in that development was the work done by the Pawnee scouts. It reminds us of the frontier that once was and has passed away.

CHAPTER I

Between the years 1860 and 1870, Columbus, on the Platte river in Nebraska, was a frontier town. It bordered on hostile Indian country. In 1864, during the first raids of the Sioux and Cheyenne war, the settlers gathered there for defense, as to a fort.

Important services in pacifying and developing this region along the Platte were performed by the North brothers. These were three sons of Thomas J. and Jane E. North, natives of Tompkins county, New York, who removed to Ohio immediately after their marriage. James E. North was born in Ohio in 1838 and Frank J. North in the state of New York in 1840, while Luther H. North was born in Ohio in the year 1846. There were two sisters, younger.

James E. North from his first coming into Nebraska, devoted himself to commercial pursuits. As a boy he was clerk in a store, and in the early day of the Colorado gold and silver excitement he worked in the mines in that territory. He thus learned much of men and their manners in different pursuits and received useful training. Later he returned to Columbus and became successful and respected as an authority on mercantile and land matters. He was of great help to a multitude of the early settlers of Nebraska who needed advice as to the method and manner of securing land. The younger brothers, Frank J. North and Luther H. North, were for some years farmers, but as frontier hunters in a country frequently invaded by hostile Indians, and by association with the friendly Pawnees, they fell into the work of fighting those hostile Indians, and thus began to make the country available for settlement and for the production of crops.

In 1855, Thomas J. North, with his eldest son, went to Omaha then the capital of the newly organized territory of Nebraska, and a year later, in the summer of 1856, his family followed him, going by steamboat from Cleveland to Chicago, thence by rail to Iowa City and finally to Council Bluffs by stage. In Omaha they found the father living on a tract of eighty acres of timber land on the borders of the town.

Mr. North was acting as agent for a landowner named Pierce, who was clearing some of his land and having the wood cut for fuel and hauled into the town. Mr. North was also having the wood cut from his land. He was a surveyor and gave part of his time to running lines for the government and laying out town sites and land claim boundaries for the settlers.

The winter of 1856-1857 was one of great severity and is still remembered as the hardest winter ever known in eastern Nebraska. The snow was six feet deep on the level and the cold very severe, so that all springs and streams were frozen. Much of the water used that winter for household purposes was from snow melted over the fire. The weather was so cold that many wild animals were killed by it. Mr. North was engaged that winter in surveying, and while laying out a town site on Papillion creek on the California emigrant trail, he was frozen to death.

The family was quite without means, and this loss left it wholly dependent on the exertions of the older sons. After his father's death, Frank took his place as agent and timekeeper for Mr. Pierce and with a yoke of oxen he owned, hauled the wood into Omaha where it was sold. J. E. North became clerk in a store in Florence, Nebraska, which at this time was making an active bid to be considered the capital of the territory. It was a busy place because of the passage through it of the westward traveling Mormons. They called the village winter quarters, and many groups stopped there, while others went on to explore the country beyond.

In 1857 J. E. North built a house in Florence and the family moved up there. The following spring, Mrs. North and her three younger children went back to New York state, remaining there for a time, and then returned to Ohio where she sold some property, stayed there through the winter, and returned to the west in the spring of 1859.

Meanwhile, the boys, James and Frank, had left Florence and had moved up the Platte valley to a point near where the town of Columbus now is. Here Frank occupied himself with his ox team in breaking up tracts of land for different settlers and during the summer planted thirty-five acres of sod corn.

9

When Mrs. North and her children returned to Omaha, she hired a man and team to take them to Columbus, which they reached sometime in the night of the second day. The first day's drive was to Fremont, then a town of six or eight log houses. Except for the stage stations, about fifteen miles apart, these were the only houses seen on the trip.

J. E. North had taken the contract to deliver the mail from Columbus to Monroe, a post office twelve miles to the westward, and his brother, Luther, carried it. He made the trip on horseback three times a week, on Tuesday, Thursday and Saturday. The country between the two settlements was mostly unoccupied and was open prairie with only a few wagon tracks to follow. It was a lonely ride for a thirteen year old boy.

The next winter while driving in the cows one evening Luther's pony slipped and fell on his leg, spraining his ankle so badly that for more than a month he could bear no weight on it; but he never missed a trip with the mail. His brother used to carry him out and put him on the pony and he would ride to Monroe where he was helped off his horse and into the house, and when the time came to start back, they carried him out and put him on his pony again.

In the autumn of 1858 three men named Messenger, MacMurray and Glass stopped in Columbus on their way west to secure wolf hides. They had a team and wagon and an outfit for trapping and poisoning wolves, which were then very numerous. They had, however, only a small supply of corn for their horses, and they proposed to Frank North that he should become a partner in the enterprise and accompany them, if he would furnish sufficient corn to feed their horses while they were on the expedition. Frank North accepted the offer and supplied the corn, and started with them. He took along a Kentucky rifle and plenty of ammunition.

Messenger was sixty years of age and had followed trapping and hunting nearly all his life. He was a silent character and hardly ever spoke to anyone. Glass was a blacksmith and MacMurray, a freighter of merchandise, which was largely whiskey which he sold secretly to the soldiers at Fort Kearney, for it was contrary to the regulations to sell liquor to troops.

Fort Phil Kearney (pronounced "car-nee") was established to protect migrants on the Bozeman Trail. On December 21, 1866, it was the site of the Fetterman Fight in which all 81 men under the command of Captain William J. Fetterman were killed by Cheyenne, Arapaho, and Sioux warriors under Red Cloud. The location today has a monument to the fallen and the site of the fort has a partially-reconstructed stockade.—Ed. 2015

The party moved westward without adventure until they reached Elm creek, where they found a suitable spot for the camp and constructed a dug-out. This was a common habitation in those and later days, and was made by digging a hole in the side of a vertical bank large enough to accommodate them all. At the rear end an oval fireplace was scooped out and a hole for a chimney dug down from the outside. The excavation was then, if necessary, roofed over with poles and brush, covered with earth. This was thus a sort of cave and made a warm, dry and comfortable shelter, affording complete protection from the severe cold of winter.

As soon as this home was made, it became necessary to kill bait for the wolves. Buffalo were numerous all about them and a few days were spent in still hunting them on foot. A number were killed and hauled into the camp where they were skinned and cut up, the best of the hides being saved. When this had been done, MacMurray returned to Omaha, Glass made an excuse for leaving and young Frank North and old Messenger were left alone at the camp. Their method of wolf poisoning was to carry out a quarter of buffalo to a point not very far from the dug-out and fasten it to the ground by driving through it a stake of ash. The wolves were large and strong and if it were not securely fastened they would drag the bait away. The meat of the buffalo quarter was poisoned with strychnine, strips were cut from it and sliced into small pieces in each of which was placed a dose of strychnine. These small poisoned baits were scattered about the quarter of meat in a large circle and left there.

The wolves smelling the meat from a distance, approached it, picking up and eating the small baits on the way and then went to the quarter and fed at that until they died from the poison. Thus all the wolf carcasses were found conveniently near to the staked down meat. In this way ten or fifteen wolves were secured every night.

There were multitudes of ravens everywhere and all of them looking for food. In order to save the wolf bait it was necessary to distribute the small pieces at night after the ravens had gone to roost. Then too the men were obliged to be afoot very early in the morning in order to begin skinning their wolves before the ravens got about. Otherwise, the hides would be destroyed by the birds. Even as it was, they lost in this way perhaps one hundred hides. Many, many hundreds of ravens were killed by eating the carcasses of the poisoned wolves.

One night, while Frank North was distributing the wolf baits, he looked behind him and saw a large white wolf following him very closely. He was somewhat startled for he was unarmed. The hungry wolf seemed to be threatening an attack and North walked pretty rapidly toward the dugout and when he had gotten within one hundred yards of it, he dropped a bit of poisoned bait. The wolf stopped to eat it and North reached the cabin. The next morning the wolf was found dead near the place Frank had left him.

Messenger and North kept at their work for six weeks. To the boy the time seemed long, for his companion was unsociable and allowed the youngster to do most of the work.

After a time Glass returned to the camp and soon after some difficulty arose between him and Messenger about some small matter of work. Nothing special was said about it, but a few days later Messenger disappeared without any warning. Glass and North continued their work, which presently was interrupted by the discovery near the cabin of a large body of mounted Indians. They were engaged in making a surround of buffalo on the Platte river and made a considerable killing, securing about five hundred buffalo. It was the custom with these Indians never to kill more buffalo than they could handle and, of course, never to frighten other herds in the neighborhood. After the killing they remained in camp for several days, until the hides had been taken off and cared for, and the meat cut up and dried for future use.

These Indians proved to be Pawnees, who were armed chiefly with bows and arrows which they handled with remarkable skill. On this occasion, as on others, a dozen or fifteen years later, they did not use guns in this killing, but depended entirely on the bows and arrows, which they shot with such force as frequently to drive an arrow clear through a buffalo. In this hunting they also used, to some extent, spears or lances, the points of which were made from old sabres, or old musket bayonets which they had procured from the whites.

Neither North nor Glass knew anything about Indians, and they were uneasy at the presence of this large party, which camped near the dug-out. They soon learned to what tribe they belonged, for not long after the surround, some of the Indians, having discovered the dug-out, rode up to inquire about it. The white men were glad to learn that they were Pawnees who were friendly, but their visitors objected strongly to the presence of the whites because, as they said, they had come into the buffalo country and were scaring the buffalo away.

Frank North could speak a few words of Pawnee which he had learned from a little group of Pawnees that had camped near the home in Omaha during the winter of 1856-57. He was thus able to talk to the Indians and explain to them the situation. To gain their friendliness, he asked them to eat with him and cooked them a good meal which the Indians greatly enjoyed. Nevertheless, before leaving, they looked at the pile of wolf hides and asked him to give them some of the best ones. The request was denied and they intimated that perhaps they would return and take the hides by force.

They went away and the two white men rather expected that they would return at night and take the property. They determined, however, to protect it, and after dark left the dug-out and hid themselves near some brush not far off. After a time a group of people were seen approaching and presently one was discovered covered by a white blanket and creeping toward the wolf hides. He looked very much as if he were a wolf. North's first impulse was to kill him, but a more discreet thought came to him, which led him to fire over the Indian, who jumped to his feet and ran off, the others following him. Nothing more was seen of them that night.

The next day several of the chiefs, among whom were Pita le sharu and Us sah wuck (Spotted Horse) came to see them. The trappers presented the chiefs with twelve buffalo skins, which seemed to give them pleasure and they went back to their camp. They probably knew nothing of the raid attempted the night before.

A little later the whole Pawnee camp moved off and they were not seen again.

About the middle of March, MacMurray returned with a team, and the wolf poisoning outfit broke up and started for Fort Kearny. They crossed the Platte river on the ice and left their hides at the fort. Soon the weather grew warm, the ice in the river broke up and the broad shallow stream became high and unfordable. They were thus unable to cross it with their wagons and were obliged to sell their hides to a trader at much less than they supposed they were worth. Messenger did not appear to claim his share of the proceeds. The trappers separated and North returned to his home in Columbus.

That spring (1859) the excitement of the Pike's Peak gold discovery rose to fever heat. North determined to make a trip to the new mining country, wither his brother, James, had already gone. He therefore bought a load of provisions and with two passengers started across the plains with a team and wagon. The broad road leading west was full of people, going and coming; the west bound teams on one of the wagon tracks and the east bound teams on the other. Those going west were full of hope, while those coming east were cast down by failure.

Notwithstanding the many discouraging reports he heard, North kept on his way and at the new town of Denver, he sold his goods at a profit. After a brief visit to his brother, who was then mining in Leavenworth Gulch, Frank returned home and spent the summer hauling freight from Omaha to Fort Kearny.

The summer of 1859 was that of the so-called Pawnee war about which much was written in those days, but most of it from hearsay and from rather uncertain memory. There were stories of active depredations by the Pawnees and of the killing of whites and Indians. General Thayer, inspired by the report, enlisted a group of volunteers who set out to punish the Pawnees. Some printed accounts of the march of his volunteers tell of the killing of several Pawnees on the way up the Elk-horn, but James E. North, who was one of the volunteers with the expedition, declared that he did not know that any Pawnees were killed, and he always believed that if the whites had attacked the Pawnees they would have been badly beaten, because they were so poorly armed. Several years afterward, Pita le sharu, the head chief of the Pawnees and always a friend of the whites, gave his version of the war. He said that some of the Pawnee young men had had trouble with the settlers near Fremont over damage that their horses had done to the growing crops, and that a cow belonging to a settler was killed by a party of Ponca Indians, but that the settlers declared that the Pawnees had killed it.

When General Thayer overtook the Indians at what is now known as Battle Creek, the Pawnees did not know what the trouble was, but Pita le sharu guessed that something was wrong and taking an American flag that had been given him in Washington two years before, he rode forward with his interpreter to meet the general, and learned he was at war with the whites. After a council with the chiefs, of which there were sixteen in the tribe, they finally turned over to General Thayer, a young man who had killed a pig belonging to a settler. The chief said that no Pawnees were killed, and that the Pawnees killed no white people.

The following autumn the Pawnees moved from their old village site near Fremont to the new reservation on the Loup, where the town of Genoa now stands. On their march from Columbus, Luther North with his mail, met them half way between Monroe and Columbus. There were three thousand of the Indians and when he saw the company the boy was badly frightened, but as he drew near the leaders, they saluted him in a friendly way and as he knew a few words of the Pawnee language, he soon learned who they were.

CHAPTER II

The first mention of the Pawnees by the whites is perhaps to be found in the account of Coronado's journey in 1541, when from Quivira he sent a message north to the "lord" of the Harahey Pawnee Indians, and somewhat later was visited by a Chief Tatarrax with two hundred warriors.

Coronado's guides to Quivira, the Turk and Ysopete, were perhaps Pawnee captives who had been living in the Pueblo village. Many years ago I heard from an old Pawnee, a tradition of a visit the tribe received from the Spaniards long, long before they had ever seen any white people from the east.

About the year 1600, Don Juan de Onate, then governor of the province of New Mexico, marched east from New Mexico and is believed to have reached the Quivirans the Pawnees whom he found to be pleasant, friendly people. They were agriculturists and cultivated corn, beans and squashes, and their homes were described as like those built by the Pawnees of comparatively recent times.

It seems likely that Onate purposed to make further exploration among the Quivirans and their relatives to the north, but news which reached him from his headquarters in New Mexico called him back there.

The detailed journal of Onate's travels has never been found, but there was published many years ago in the Diario Official in the city of Mexico, what purported to be an account of everything that has been seen and known in New Mexico from the year 1538 till 1625 by Father Salmeron, a missionary priest among the Pueblos for eight years, during which time he probably wrote this volume.

In the last of the seventeenth century, the French and Spanish were competing for the control of the southern plains country and its inhabitants. Their anxiety for this control sprang from very different motives. The Canadian French, who had extended their journeyings out on to the northeastern plains, were trappers and traders and were keenly interested in the fur trade. The Spanish on the other hand seem to have cared little about the fur trade, but were chiefly anxious for the souls of the Indians, wishing to send priests among them and to accomplish a general conversion. Obviously, at that early day neither nation had any interest whatever in the settlement of the west nor in its economic development.

In the latter part of that century, the French were active in what are now the southwestern United States and there is little doubt that some of them were already with the Pawnees. Certainly they were with them in the next century and in 1720 the expedition of Villazur, comprising fifty Spanish soldiers with some Apache allies, was sent north from Santa Fe, in order to negotiate with the Pawnees, and to drive away any Frenchmen that might be with them. Villazur found the Pawnee village near the forks of the Platte river, where he was attacked by the Pawnees, probably aided by the French and he and most of the soldiers of his command were killed and all their property captured.

At that time the territory occupied by the Pawnees extended from the Niobrara river on the north ,south to beyond Arkansas and almost from the Missouri river on the east, west beyond the forks of the Platte river. This included, of course, the heads of the Republican river, which was a great buffalo country. Even within recent years, the Cheyenne Indians used to speak of the country about old Fort Kearny, including the heads of the Republican river, as Pawnee country, into which they dared not venture.

At the beginning of the nineteenth century, Spain and the United States were not on very friendly terms. The Spanish suspected that the United States wished to encroach on territory which Spain claimed as hers, while the United States was sending out men to explore those lands that this country had recently purchased from France. The territorial boundaries of those days were altogether vague.

In 1806, the Spanish government sent out from New Mexico a large party of troops under Lieutenant Don Facundo Malgares—or Melgares to descend the Red river of the south, in order to turn back any United States expedition that might be exploring it, to examine the interior of the country from the frontiers of the province of New

Mexico to the Missouri and to make friends with the various Indian tribes which occupied that country. This expedition of something like six hundred men and two thousand animals came down the Red river, a long distance, met the Comanche Indians, and talked with them, then struck off northeast and crossing the Arkansas river, came to the Pawnee villages. Here the commander talked with these people and presented to them Spanish flags and medals, and after a time returned to Santa Fe.

Not very long after the visit to the Pawnees by Lieutenant Malgares, Lieutenant Zebulon M. Pike reached the Pawnee village and held a grand council with the Pawnees. Pike told them in substance that they were under the government of the United States and not under that of Spain, and demanded that the Spanish flag, which hung at the door of the Pawnee chief, should be taken down and delivered to him and that the flag of the United States should be received and hoisted to its place. Pike recognized that this demand was rather daring. It was only a short time since a force of at least three hundred Spanish cavalrymen had been at the village, greatly impressing the Indians by their display, while Pike himself had but about twenty men on foot. The Pawnee chief in his response to Pike made no allusion to his demand for the flag. Pike then repeated what he had said, adding, "that it was impossible for a nation to have two Fathers; that they must either be the children of the Spaniards, or acknowledge their American Father." After he had finished speaking there was still hesitancy, but at last an old man took down the Spanish flag and delivered it to Pike who gave him the American flag which was then hoisted.

Nevertheless, the Pawnees doubtful, and perhaps fearful of what might be done to them by the Spaniards, if they should return, were downcast and sorrowful. Pike tactfully soothed their fears by returning to them the Spanish flag with the understanding that during Pike's stay it should not again be hoisted. This gave great satisfaction to the Pawnees.

In Major Sibley's diary, written in the year 1811, is found a note on Pike's visit to the Pawnees. This has a peculiar interest because it gives certain details about the visit, which purport to come from the

Pawnees themselves. These details seem to explain statements made by Pike, on which he does not enlarge. Anyone who is familiar with Indians and with, the way in which they look at things can readily understand the point of view of the Pawnee chief whose acts are described. Except honesty, there is nothing that the primitive Indian respects so much as he respects courage and for this reason it is not surprising that the Pawnee chief acted as he did. He seemed too to be impressed by the difference between the mental attitude of Pike and his men and that of the Spanish expedition which had been sent north to punish the Skiris, but was easily persuaded not to attack them. Writing generally of the Pawnees, Major Sibley says:

"They sometimes push their predatory excursions to the Spanish settlements of New Mexico. The Loups or Ske-nees (Skiris) committed such serious depredations there a few years ago, as induced the Governor of that province to send a strong detachment of mounted militia to their town to chastise them or, as the old Chief told me, 'to kill them all.' The commander of this detachment consulted Cher-a-ta-reesh on his arrival at the Republican town, and was by him (so he told me) persuaded to spare the Ske-nees, which I presume the old warrior found it easy enough to do. In a few days after this Spanish Rabble had left the Pawnees, Lieutenant Z. M. Pike arrived there with his exploring party of about twenty-five men including Lieutenant Wilkinson (son of General Wilkinson) and Dr. John A. Robinson. Lieutenant Pike stayed several days, recruiting his party, purchasing horses and was treated kindly. When he announced his intention of pursuing his journey towards the Spanish settlements, the old Chief promptly objected and said he had promised the Spanish officer who had just been there to prevent any American party from passing through his country towards New Mexico, and that he must redeem his promise. Pike replied that his Chief had ordered him to go; go he would or die in the attempt.

"'Why/ said Cher-a-ta-reesh, 'you have only twenty-five warriors here, and I can command a thousand and have them here in less than half a day; how then can you go if I forbid it? You are a brave young warrior, and your men are all braves also, but what can so few do? I respect you, I love you, I love you as my own son. I love brave men. Do not oblige me to hurt you; you must not pass.' Still Pike persisted and having all things ready, solemnly announced to the chief that on the following morning he should pursue his journey to the

Mexican mountains, at the same time thanking him for his hospitality. The morning came and the rising sun found Pike with his men all mounted, well-armed and equipped, their broad swords drawn.

"The old warrior Chief had summoned his forces also, and there they stood (more than 500 in number) armed with bows and arrows, spears and tomahawk in gloomy silence, each party waiting the order of their Chief.

"Cher-a-ta-reesh, unarmed and on foot, approached closer to the side of Pike and with much emotion urged him to desist, but in vain; pointing to the sun and to a small speck in the sky just above, 'Brave Chief,' said he [Pike] 'When the sun reaches you point in his daily journey, I shall surely set out upon mine. I will start, I and my brave comrades here and nothing but death can stop us; it is my duty, as I have told you. If you think it yours to obey the Spaniard and to stop me, be it so, but the attempt will cost the lives of some brave men, that you may be sure of.'

"Not two minutes remained, the Chief stood in thoughtful silence whilst Pike addressed his own men, all was ready, the soldiers were bracing themselves firmly in their saddles, the Indian warriors had strung their bows and some had fixed their arrows (more sure and deadly than bullets). Pike's hand grasped his sword hilt, yet in its scabbard (it being drawn was the appointed signal for the onset, for his whole party was surrounded by Pawnees).

"'What a moment!' In a few minutes, perhaps a hundred brave men would bite the dust. One word from the Pawnee Chief was only wanting to prevent this waste of human life. The humanity of the good old Chief prevailed. He ordered his people to open the way, to put up their weapons and let the little band pass freely and go unmolested in whatever direction their Chief chose to lead them, then turning to Pike, he said, 'Brave young Chief, you are free to pursue your journey; were I now to stop you by destroying you, the only way I am convinced that it can be done, I should forever after feel myself a coward. But Cher-a-ta-reesh is no coward, no man alive dare call me so, but the brave love those who are brave. The Spanish Chief with more than 500 men seemed afraid to strike the Ske-nees though they had robbed them. I only whispered in his ear a few words and he went home again as he came. If he wishes to stop you he may do it himself, Cher-a-ta-reesh will no longer interfere.'

"After some friendly adieus, Pike and his men set forward in order at a brisk gait and soon left the Pawnees out of sight but not out of mind, for they loved to speak of the brave Americans.

"I have given you these incidents just as they were related to me by the Great Pawnee Chief. He further told me as in connection, that during Pike's stay in his village he had surrendered to him at his request all his Spanish medals and flags, upon his promise that they would be replaced by others from his great American father, but he had not yet seen or heard anything about them. He feared they were forgotten. All this conversation about Pike, you must understand, took place the morning after I reached the Pawnees, and whilst I lay on my pallet in the Chief's lodge, and before I had entered upon any business, or even told why I had visited him and his people. Nothing could have suited the occasion better than this previous communication from the Chief about my friend Pike and his promise of medals and flags, all entirely new to me or to any other agent of the Government. Not one word of the whole story did I doubt the truth of. Now, as my main business at the Pawnees was to let them know exactly what were their relations with our Government and that their former dependence on and allegiance to the Spanish authorities in New Mexico was entirely dissolved, I had taken care to provide myself well with American Flags and medals, to make use of, as occasion might require. As soon as the old Chief had concluded his narration which he wound up by telling me about the medals and flags Lieutenant Pike had promised him, I seized on the coincidence (I think justifiably) not only to aid my own views, but also at the same time to vindicate Pike, and pay his promises. I therefore quickly informed the Chief that the medals and flags were then actually there and should be delivered, sick as I was, on that very day if he desired it. He said he was satisfied that I had brought them and would wait till I got over my headache and felt well again, for their delivery and in the meantime would announce the facts to the Pawnees, and so he did. Criers were sent around to tell the news that the stranger just arrived was the brother of the 'brave young American Chief' (they all knew Pike by that name) and had brought with him the promised medals and flags. Feeling much better in the evening, I unpacked my baggage, selected three handsome flags, one for each tribe in the Town, and presented them to Cher-a-ta-reesh and they were waving high over the village in a very short time. I also sent one to the Ske-nee Town. On the last day of May I held a grand council with all the Chiefs and head men of both towns, four tribes, and then after due inquiry as to fit persons, distributed a number of medals of various sizes.

"It was very natural for the Pawnee Chief to be less reserved towards me after he had identified me with Lieutenant Pike whom he so much admired, when he introduced me to his peoples, as the brother of Pike, he meant and was so understood, merely to say that I was his countryman, and the old man seemed to think it sufficient honor for any man to be called the Countryman of Pike

CHAPTER III

In the middle of the last century, the Pawnees were one of the best known of our Western tribes. Missionaries had been with them since the early part of the century; some groups had had their villages on the Missouri river, not far from St. Louis and their homes on and near the Platte river were directly in the line of emigration to the West, which began about the year 1840.

It was this emigration, more than anything else, which marked the beginning of the downfall of the Pawnees, for it introduced to these Indians, who up to that time had been more or less apart, the white man's diseases and the white man's liquor. The Pawnees had no tribal friends on the prairie. They were real Ishmaelites and were subject to constant attack by the Dakotas on the east and the north, the Cheyenne and Kiowa on the north and west and the Comanche and Wichita on the south.

On the other hand, the Pawnees have always been friendly with the whites. Rarely one may read of an attack on some emigrant train by a band of Pawnees, but such attacks when made, were usually conducted by groups of young men who were trying to take the travelers' horses and not as an act of war against the whites, but rather as stealing possessions that belonged to others for the purpose of increasing their own. Such an occurrence was in no sense a racial attack, but may rather be compared with the act of the pickpocket or burglar who is engaged in practicing his vocation in a civilized community. The Pawnees were famous for their skill and success in capturing horses from their enemies. In those days horses were the most valuable property on the prairie and could be exchanged for any desirable thing. For this reason no one could have too many horses and everyone was constantly trying to add to the number he possessed.

The traditions of the Pawnees declare they first came from the extreme southwest, somewhere down in Mexico and possibly from the shores of the gulf of California. This migration took place in the distant past and there is no way of fixing a date for it. We are told that when it took place, the migrating horde was very great. It must not be understood, however, that this was the movement of a great body of people together. It was rather a slow journey made by a great number of small groups. In such a migration, the most important question would obviously be that of food. Of this food a part would be the wild game and the native roots, but in the case of the Pawnee groups who have always cultivated the ground, we may conceive that the movement was very slow and that pauses covering considerable time would occur at frequent intervals for the purpose of raising crops and the accumulation of food sufficient to permit another forward movement.

These groups of migrating people crossed the Rio Grande and moved northeast and east, passing over what is now Texas and getting as far east as Louisiana.

When the ancestors of the Pawnees started on their long migration from the south, they knew nothing of horses. Their journeying was on foot and their possessions were carried on the backs of the people, except so far as their dogs bore small packs on their backs or hauled loads on the travois.

Tribal tradition declares that on their way to the north, men who were traveling far ahead of one of the groups saw from the top of a hill a body of people that had with them large four-legged animals unlike any known to the Pawnees. The scouts reported their discovery to the chiefs who were behind with the main company, and a council was had as to how these newly discovered people should be met-whether as friends or as enemies. It was decided to attack them. This was done; the Pawnees driving the strangers from the field and capturing the animals they possessed. These were horses, the first that the Pawnees had ever seen and they did not understand for what purpose they could be used. They learned later to ride and to pack them.

The tradition adds that the people from whom these horses were taken were Sioux and Cheyennes, but this is an erroneous notion based on modern war experience and modern feelings. At the distant day when this must have occurred there were no Sioux or Cheyennes in the west. If the tradition of the attack is based on fact, it no doubt took place far to the south, where there were more horses than in the north country, toward which the Pawnees were journeying.

In this connection it may be remembered that among the Pawnees there is a tradition that the first horseman they ever saw was a man riding a mule and that those who saw this, supposed man and mule to be a single animal—the old idea of the centaur held also by the Mexicans when they saw the horsemen of Cortez.

Many tribes belonged to this Caddoan stock, which takes its name from one of the earliest known tribes. Familiar tribal names are Arikara, Pawnee, Wichita, or Pawnee Piet, Caddo, Hueco, Kcechie and Tawa-conie. Of these tribes, the Arikara lived farthest to the north—well up on the Missouri river the Skiri on the Loup Fork, and the Pawnees on the Platte river; while the other tribes lived further south in Kansas, the Indian Territory, Louisiana and Texas.

All these groups were long ago moved from their earlier homes and are now on various Indian reservations. All are greatly reduced in numbers, and some have even forgotten their own traditions.

Since this migration took place in prehistoric times, no one can know how long the Pawnees have lived in the country which they occupied during most of the nineteenth century. Evidently, their stay there was a long one, so long that the meanings of certain Pawnee words have changed to fit the territory. Thus, two Pawnee words which signify up-stream and downstream, respectively, came in the later Pawnee language to mean west and east, because in the country they inhabited all the streams flowed from the west to the east. In the same way, a word meaning "toward the Wichitas" came to mean south, because the Pawnees had lived so long in the country north of that occupied by the Wichitas. Such changes in the meanings of words require time.

Pawnee place names had been given to many of the natural features of the region. Here is the story of one place name: In a battle between Sioux and Pawnees which took place long ago, somewhere near where the city of Cheyenne now stands, the Pawnees were obliged to retreat before the greater number of the Sioux, who drove them south into Colorado. The Pawnees finally took refuge near Crow creek in some high bluffs which are almost vertical on all sides except one, where the Pawnees went up and then turned to defend the passage. The Sioux did not venture to attack them here, but guarded the way up the bluff to prevent the escape of the Pawnees, feeling sure that it would be impossible for them to climb down the steep walls. During the days of the siege, the Pawnees suffered greatly from lack of food and water and the only prospect before them was death, either at the hands of their enemies or through starvation. One dark night, however, they tied together a number of their ropes and fastened one end of the line on top of the bluff and let it down over the almost vertical side in the hope that it might reach the ground below. By the help of this rope one man slowly descended, digging footholds as he could, with his knife in the hard smooth clay. He finally reached the ground below and signaling to his companions with the rope in a manner previously agreed upon, they let themselves down one by one and all reached the ground in safety and escaped.

From that time forward these bluffs were called the Pawnee Buttes and a little stream known as Pawnee creek flows from their base and enters the Platte river, west of Julesburg. A story similar to this is told of Court House Rock, as I have elsewhere said. Such an event might well enough have happened more than once.

It has been suggested that this story is doubtful, because on their horse stealing expeditions the Pawnees carried small horse hair ropes for use on the horses they took, and such ropes would not be strong enough to support the weight of men let down for a long distance. It is true that the Pawnees like other Indian tribes did carry these hair ropes, but they carried also ropes of rawhide which could be used in the manner suggested by the story. Because of its lightness a horse hair rope cannot be used for throwing at a distance and heavier ropes would probably be needed for catching horses. The tradition seems at least worth mentioning.

Of the tribe which we have known as Pawnees, there are four sub-tribes or bands, and seventy-five or one hundred years ago, the best estimate of the numbers of this tribe was from ten thousand to twelve thousand five hundred individuals. These sub-tribes are the

Skiri or Wolf, the Tsaui or Grand, the Kit ka hah ki or Republican, and the Pita hau i rat, Tapage or Noisy.

In 1834, the Pawnee agent, Major Dougherty, estimated their numbers at twelve thousand five hundred, but a few years after that, the tribes suffered greatly from smallpox. Since that time, their numbers have been decreasing, until in 1879 they were thought to be only fourteen hundred and forty people, and 1906 about six hundred and fifty. At present, they number but a few hundred.

The first treaty between the Pawnees and the United States was made in June, 1818, and this was followed by one in 1825, acknowledging the supremacy of the United States. In October, 1833, the Pawnees ceded all their land south of the Platte river and in 1848 sold a great strip of land on the Platte, near Grand Island. In 1857, all lands north of the Platte river were assigned to the United States, except a strip on the Loup river, thirty miles by fifteen, where their reservation was established. In 1859 they moved from their old village at Pahuk on the south side of the Platte river near Fremont, Nebraska, to the village on the Loup river, near where the town of Genoa now stands. In 1876 they ceded to the United States the Loup river area.

For a long time the relationship between the Wichitas and the Pawnees had been forgotten and the two tribes were actively at war until about 1868, when Running Chief, a Kit ka hah ki warrior, by an act of great bravery so impressed the Wichita chief and warriors that they proposed that there should be no more war between the two tribes and that the road between their villages be made white. "Let it no more show any spot of blood."

Two or three years later such a peace was made by the Pawnees, and not only with the Wichitas, but with the Kiowa and Comanches as well.

During the summer of 1873 the Pawnees went on their buffalo hunt to the Republican valley. The hunt was successful and they were returning to the Platte river when the marching column of women and children was attacked by a large party of Sioux, at a time when the Pawnee men were off hunting. About one hundred and fifty women and children were killed.

In the winter of 1873 and 1874 two Pawnee men of some standing, Frank White and Big Spotted Horse, went south to the Indian Territory to visit the Wichitas. These said that they wished the Pawnees to move south to the Indian Territory and to live near them. They urged the visitors to try to persuade the Pawnees to move and promised White and Big Spotted Horse handsome presents if they could bring this about.

The two returned to the agency on the Loup river and reached there just as the Pawnees were receiving their annuity payments from Major Burgess, the agent, and Barclay White, Superintendent of Indian affairs, in Nebraska. They reported on their visit to the south and delivered to the Pawnees the invitation from the Wichitas. At a council held a little later they praised in glowing terms the hospitality of the Wichitas and described the Indian Territory as a beautiful country. They asked the superintendent and agent to intercede with the Great Father at Washington to obtain a relinquishment of the Pawnee rights in Nebraska, and secure for them a tract of land in the Indian Territory. The chiefs of the tribe strongly objected to this proposition and denounced these two men, who, they declared, were trying to deceive the people. On the other hand the flattering statements regarding the Indian Territory were received with considerable enthusiasm by a majority of the tribe, who were inclined to accept the invitation of the Wichitas, although not one acknowledged chief was in favor of it.

The next day in a talk with the Indians, Superintendent White found that a majority wished to go to the Indian Territory, notwithstanding the opposition of the chiefs. He declared that he would obtain for Frank White and Big Spotted Horse a transfer from Washington. The transfer came in a short time and by it the two were permitted to emigrate to the Indian Territory and to take with them all those who wished to accompany them. When they were ready to start it was found that almost three-fourths of the tribe wished to go. They took their own ponies and Superintendent White sent with them a government employee to supervise their movement. All the chiefs and their families remained at the old home.

The Pawnees reached the Wichita agency and met with a cordial reception. They settled on the Arkansas river in the southern part of the Indian Territory, about forty miles from Fort Sill. The friendly tribes in the neighborhood made good their promises by presenting to the Pawnees eight or nine hundred horses and other valuable presents. When the report of this generous action reached the ears of the Pawnee chiefs who had remained in the north, it no doubt had some influence on them. Although all were very reluctant to leave their old home, they finally reached the conclusion that it would be better for all to move down to the Indian Territory. After they had reached this determination, congress made an appropriation of $150,000 to cover the expense of moving the tribe, and $150,000 for the erection of agency buildings in the Indian Territory. In the fall of 1874, they started for their new home.

While crossing the Loup Fork, old Pita le sharu, the head chief, was shot in the knee by the accidental discharge of his pistol. The wound was a severe one and the Indians went into camp until he should recover sufficiently to be able to travel. The old chief thought the accident a bad omen. He predicted that he would soon die, that the tribe would suffer great loss of life and that they would regret the move they were now making. Doctors called from Columbus to attend him said that he would probably recover from his wound, but in a few days he died.

The Pawnees went on to the Indian Territory. They chose there a reservation between the Arkansas and Cimarron rivers and located their agency on Black Bear creek. Here they were soon joined by the section of the tribe that had preceded them. During the first eighteen months of the residence of the Pawnees in the Indian Territory the prediction of Pita le sharu came true. Many of the people, including four-fifths of all the prominent chiefs and leading men of the tribe, died and for years afterwards there was much sickness among them. For a long time after this the Pawnees believed these misfortunes to be a visitation of the Great Spirit to punish them for their failure to listen to their leaders.

In 1892 the Pawnees took their lands in severalty and became citizens of the United States.

CHAPTER IV

In the autumn of 1860, Frank North secured employment at the Pawnee reservation under the agent named De Puy. Shortly after this, his brother Luther went to the agency, and the two were engaged in hauling wood and logs to the saw-mill that the government had built for the Indians.

In the spring of 1861 a new man, named Luschbaugh, took the place of the previous Pawnee agent, and a son-in-law of the commissioner of Indian affairs was appointed trader for the Pawnees. This trader, named Rudy, learning that Frank North could speak the Pawnee language fluently, employed him as interpreter and clerk at the trading post. Rudy lived in Illinois and except for his visits to the agency each spring and fall, when the Indians received their annuities, North was left in entire charge of the business.

The year 1861 was marked by a number of raids by the Sioux Indians on the Pawnee reservation, and in one of those Luther North had rather a narrow escape, of which I will let him tell in his own words:

"After the grass had well started, we used to turn out our horses and mules at night to graze. One morning they were gone. I jumped on a little saddle mule, bare-back, to hunt for them. I had no idea they would be far off, so did not take with me either a gun or revolver. I rode along the foot of the hill looking up every ravine

I came to, till I had gone about a mile and had made up my mind to turn back, when a band of Sioux Indians rode over the hill. They were between me and the agency buildings, and I could not run in that direction, but south of me about a mile lived Mr. H. J. Hudson, a trader, and I rode for his place. The Sioux followed me, but after chasing me for perhaps half a mile, they turned toward a field where some Pawnee women were hoeing corn, all except one man who kept after me. He was armed with bow and arrows and a long lance, and was riding a fast horse that was gaining on me at every jump. I was riding that mule hard and he was doing his very best, but it was hardly good enough. We were about a quarter of a mile from the trading-post and the Indian was just about ready to drive his lance into me, when his horse stepped into a prairie-dog hole and fell. Before the Sioux could get to his feet and use his bow and arrows, I was safe, but the poor Pawnee women were not so lucky. Nine of them were killed and one of them that was running for the trading post was caught and scalped by the man that had chased me. He ran up to her, caught her by the hair with his left hand and cut a piece about four inches square off the top of her head. He did not get off his horse. We were shooting at him, but the guns we used were some old muskets that had been given the Pawnees, and were as likely to burst and kill the shooter as to harm anyone who stood in front of them.

"In the race I lost my straw hat, and about a month later Adam Smith, who was freighting to Cottonwood Springs, saw a party of Sioux Indians at Fort Kearny and one of them was wearing my hat! They belonged to the Brule Sioux under Spotted Tail, and at that time were not at war with the whites, but that would not stop them from killing white men on the Pawnee reservation. Adam Smith was killed by the same band of Sioux in 1864, while putting up hay for the Government near the Pawnee reservation."

As soon as the attack became known, the Pawnee warriors sprang on their horses and set out in pursuit of the enemy. During a running fight, the Pawnees killed a number of Sioux. Again in the autumn, the Sioux attacked the Pawnees, killing the official interpreter. In this fight the Sioux were driven off with a loss of eleven warriors. These attacks by the Sioux became so frequent and annoying that in the spring of 1863 a company of the Second Nebraska cavalry was sent to the reservation.

In the fall of 1862, Luther North enlisted in the Second Nebraska cavalry. They were mustered in at Omaha and wintered at the Pawnee reservation. In the spring of 1863 they marched across the country to Sioux City, Iowa, and joined the expedition against the Indians under General Alfred Sully. There were two regiments of cavalry, the Iowa Sixth and the Nebraska Second. The transportation was one hundred eighty mule teams.

About one thousand of the mules were unbroken when they came to Sioux City. As the regiment was in camp there for three or four weeks, the teamsters spent the time in breaking them, but they were still pretty wild when they started up the river. One day a little dog belonging to the Colonel, Robert W. Furniss, ran up to one of the teams and began to bark. The mules got scared, the saddle mule began to buck and threw his rider and the team ran away. As they passed the team in front of them, that also ran away. In about five minutes pretty nearly every one of the one hundred eighty teams were running away, and before they were all caught they had scattered flour, sugar, coffee, bacon and beans over a large part of Dakota territory. The damage done was so serious that the column went into camp and it took about two weeks to gather up the wreckage and repair the wagons and harnesses, so that they could again move.

The regiment was armed with long-barreled muzzle loading Springfield rifles, and the revolvers were Colts, calibre .44 also muzzle loaders. Besides these firearms the regulation sabre was worn. It took a pretty expert horseman to load one of these long rifles; especially if his horse was not perfectly gentle. They tried drilling the men on horseback, but the guns were so awkward that most of the drilling was done on foot.

The command marched up the Missouri river as far as old Fort Pierre, then across country to the head of the James river, and on September 3, 1863, the Indians were overtaken and fought at White Stone Hills, in what is now North Dakota. The Indians discovered the force before it reached the village and ran away, leaving their lodges standing, but after a chase of several miles they were overtaken and surrounded in a ravine.

The Indian fighting was not very serious, though a few soldiers were killed. General Sully's report stated that something over one hundred Indians were killed and one hundred and fifty-six taken prisoner. Shortly after this battle the command returned to the Missouri river and went down it until the Crow Creek Indian agency was reached, where part of it was left to guard the Santee Sioux and the Winnebago Indians. After a time it was ordered to Omaha and mustered out about December, 1863.

In the autumn of 1863 a party of three hundred Sioux under Little Thunder made an attack on the Pawnees. A Pawnee woman was scalped and the military commander who happened to be at the agency with agent Luschbaugh, set out in pursuit of the man who had scalped the woman. These two white men followed him for a mile or more and then discovered that they were surrounded by Indians. They did not know whether these were Sioux or Pawnees, but supposed the latter. Presently, they discovered that the Indians were Sioux and so presumably hostile, and when they learned this, they rode back to the Agency. The captain had received a trifling arrow wound. A running fight followed between the Pawnees, white employees and cavalrymen on one side and the Sioux on the other. A white soldier was killed and another wounded, and seven or eight Pawnees were killed, as well as a number of Sioux.

The Pawnee woman scalped near the agency, proved to have been unwounded except for the scalping, but the Pawnees believed that a person who had been scalped was practically dead. When her people found that this woman was alive, they took her away and buried her up to her neck in the ground in an old Mormon cellar. They put a covering over her head and went away leaving her to die. Three or four days later, Mrs. Platt, the school teacher at the agency, while passing this cellar, heard a groan and on looking about discovered the Indian woman and had her brought to the agency. Food was given her, her head was dressed and after two or three weeks she was greatly improved, and seemed on the way to recovery. Mrs. Platt then asked the agent to compel her people to take care of her and the chiefs on receiving the orders consented to do so, and the next day carried her away from the mill where she had been convalescing. She was not seen again, but sometime afterward the chiefs reported that she was doing very well. The two Indians who took the woman away, instead of taking her to her family, killed her on the bank of the stream and sunk her body in a deep eddy, placing large flat stones on it to keep it down. The Indians, who had great confidence in him, told North of the manner in which she had been disposed of. He never told anyone of the matter until years afterward, well knowing that to report the occurrence would do no good.

During 1864 Luther North did much freighting between Columbus and Fort Kearny and some of this was in the winter during bitter cold weather. One noon in mid-summer, while he was returning down the Platte river, a band of thirty or forty Indians rode out of the river and up to him. He paid no particular attention to them, because most Indians were friendly, but instead of asking him for something to eat, they began to circle around the wagon in a threatening way, shouting the war cry. He saw that they were much excited and though he was familiar with Indians and Indian ways, he was a little doubtful as to what was to happen. Presently, a young man rode up in front of him, stopped his horse, fitted an arrow to his bow, pointed it at his breast and pulled it back almost to the head. While the man was doing this, another Indian rode up to him, shouting and making signs and struck the arrow aside. They talked excitedly for a few minutes and it was evident that some of them wished to kill him and others were opposed to this. Presently they turned and all rode off toward the river, and North hitched up his team and started on. He could see on the other side of the river a large Indian camp moving south, and it was probably the fact that these women and children were in the neighborhood that kept the Indians from killing him. Some soldiers were camped at or near the Cottonwood Springs afterward Fort McPherson-and the Indians felt that if they began hostilities before the women and children had been moved to a safe place, their families might be in danger. The second night after they met Luther North, the Indians made a raid on some emigrants near Plum creek, and killed all the people in the train fourteen of them.

This was one of the first raids of the Great Sioux war, which began in the summer of 1864. The Sioux declared that they had been wronged by their agent and that their treaty stipulations had been disregarded. There were twenty-five or thirty bands of Sioux of which the Brules and Ogallalas were the most numerous and important.

When it became known that the Sioux had declared war, the settlers became generally alarmed and many of them deserted their farms and ranches and flocked into the small towns for safety. The town of Columbus was protected by a stockade and all the settlers in the vicinity moved in for protection, bringing their livestock with them. The horses, cattle and a few sheep and hogs were kept inside the stockade at night and during the day were turned out and herded along the river. Two companies of militia were organized, one of cavalry and one of infantry and a night patrol was kept up by the infantrymen within the stockade and by the cavalrymen outside. A company of Federal cavalry was sent to Columbus, but as no attack was made, after a time, the excitement died down and the people began moving back to their farms. It was about this time that Luther North did his first scouting for the government.

It had been reported that another company of cavalry was to cross the Missouri river at Dakota City to be stationed at Columbus, while the company then there was to be moved to another place. The quartermaster at Columbus could not hear anything from the troops that were expected, and wished to get someone to ride across the country and guide them to Columbus. Luther North was asked to go, and rode over to Dakota City alone, making the trip in three days. There he found that the company had taken an old trail that led to Genoa, instead of to Columbus. The troops had been gone four days when he discovered this and he returned to Columbus and was on the trail another three days. The troops had not reached there and in explaining to Lieutenant Robley why he had not followed the troops to Genoa, North predicted that they would be in the next day about noon. This proved to be a good guess, for at that time they appeared.

In 1864, Frank North was sent out by the trader at the Pawnee agency to accompany some of the troops that were going to Fort Kearny. These were the Twelfth and Sixteenth Kansas cavalry and a company of the Second Nebraska cavalry. General Curtis, who was in command, took a fancy to Frank North and when he learned that he had lived among and knew well the Pawnees, he suggested that he organize a company of Pawnee scouts for the campaign.

36

Frank North knew the Pawnees to be good warriors and bitterly hostile to the Sioux and felt that such an organization might be very helpful. He therefore took with him a man named McFadden, who had been an interpreter at the Pawnee agency and who also had been with General Harney in the Ash Hollow fight in 1856. With the authority to raise a company of scouts, North and McFadden went to the Pawnees and enlisted seventy-seven young men. The Pawnees furnished their own horses and with their white leaders rode to Fort Kearny. Because of his previous military service, McFadden was chosen captain of the group, and North first lieutenant.

The enlistment of Indians in the army service was then a new idea, and the officers at Fort Kearny were much interested in this group of scouts, and curious to see how they would conduct themselves. When enlisted, they were promised the pay of cavalrymen, as well as a certain sum each for furnishing their own horses. Although they served through the campaign, they never received any pay.

Fort Kearny was a six-company post and, like most of the military posts or forts of that day, consisted of a group of frame structures for officers, men and horses. There was no enclosure or stockade. At Fort Kearny ten days were spent in organizing the expedition and then a force of one hundred and eighty men under General S. R. Curtis set out for Plum creek. A part of the expedition was made up of details from the First Nebraska cavalry, Seventh Iowa cavalry and Second Nebraska cavalry. There was a large wagon train.

At Plum creek the command left the Platte river and turned south, crossing the Republican at the mouth of Turkey creek and going on south to the Solomon river in Kansas, where frequent raids on the white settlers were being made by the Sioux. On the Solomon river, General Mitchell took command of the Second Nebraska cavalry and the Seventh Iowa cavalry with some of the Pawnee scouts under McFadden, while General Curtis with the Kansas cavalry and the First Nebraska cavalry under Colonel Livingston and the remainder of the Pawnee scouts moved down the Solomon river toward Fort Riley. Sixty-miles west of Fort Riley the frightened settlers had come together from the surrounding country and built a stockade within which they were living, awaiting an attack by the Indians who had already killed a number of persons.

This group of settlers begged General Curtis to leave with them enough troops to protect them, but Curtis did not feel that he could spare any of his force, though he gave them a one pound rifled Parrot gun to use in defending their stockade. From this point the command went on to Fort Riley, where Curtis received dispatches advising him of the advance from the south of the Rebel general, Price, with a large force. General Curtis turned over the command to Colonel Livingston, and, taking his Kansas troops with his body-guard and staff, made a forced march down the Kansas river and met and drove off Price.

During the march from the Platte to the Solomon river, General Curtis had several times noticed that McFadden did not seem to exercise control over the Pawnees. He learned that McFadden instead of ordering his men out on a scout, went amongst them and asked different ones if they were willing to go. Asked in this way, the Pawnees did not consider that they were receiving orders and sometimes did not go, or if they went, they did not feel it imperative to make a careful search of the country. Their scouting expeditions were therefore unsatisfactory, and General Curtis tried the experiment of giving all his instructions to Lieutenant North, who ordered the Pawnees out and saw that his orders were obeyed.

As a result of Frank North's handling of this group of scouts under General Curtis in 1864, that officer gave him authority to enlist a company of one hundred Pawnee scouts. He was to have the rank of captain and the organization was to be known as the Pawnee scouts. This organization was to be equipped and uniformed like other cavalry soldiers and to be brought together at Fort Kearny. North requested that McFadden be made one of his lieutenants, but his recent experience led General Curtis to refuse.

At the end of this campaign, Frank North and all the Pawnee scouts returned to their reservation, reaching there in October. Three days afterward North called a council of the tribe, told them of the instructions given him by General Curtis and said that he wished to enlist one hundred good able-bodied warriors for one year's

38

service. In less than one hour he had enrolled one hundred capable Pawnee warriors, all of whom were anxious to go on the warpath against their old enemies, the Sioux.

CHAPTER V

The Pawnee battalion was recruited from the best warriors of the tribe. It was a body of fighting men well fitted for work against the hostile Sioux and Cheyennes. When North advised General Mitchell that he had recruited a full company of Pawnees and was awaiting instructions, he was directed to come to Omaha with a list of the Indians' names. There was then no railroad and North was obliged to ride into Omaha, making the trip in three days. He reported to the mustering officer, Captain Wilcox, Fourth United States cavalry, but Wilcox was busy and delayed North from day to day for two weeks. Finally he was given a hearing, furnished with a muster roll and enlistment papers and ordered to return to the agency, and formally to enlist one hundred Pawnee warriors for one year. When he reached Columbus he learned that the Pawnees had started on their winter buffalo hunt and all those who had agreed to enlist had gone with them. Frank North was obliged to return at once to Omaha and he asked his brother, Luther, to follow the tribe and persuade the men he had enlisted to return.

Accompanied by a young Pawnee boy, Luther, who was then eighteen years old, following the trail of the Pawnee camp to where Grand Island now is, crossed the Platte river and went south to the Little Blue river. Here they were caught in a blizzard that lasted for three days, and when the storm was over the trail was covered with snow and could not be followed. The two boys, being out of provisions, started back again. They were four days on the way, during which time they had nothing to eat and the weather was very cold. When they reached the Silver creek on the third day, the stream was frozen, the ice very smooth and the horses barefooted, so that they could not cross. They went down the stream and found a place where the ice was partly covered with snow to within about one hundred yards of the north bank of the river. Beyond the snow, the ice was smooth as glass, but the Indian boy chopped a hole in the ice where he could reach the bottom and began to scoop up handfuls of wet sand and throw it on the ice. It was surprising how little it took to roughen the ice so that the ponies could walk on it. Somewhat later they came to the Loup river, and leaving their horses, crossed over to the North house where they procured a spade and returned to the river and built a sand path across the ice for the horses.

Later Frank North, accompanied by a Pawnee guide and Charles A. Small, the agent's private secretary, set out to find the Pawnees. They did not succeed in finding them and after a long journey and some suffering from the lack of food they returned to Columbus. Here a telegram was awaiting Captain North, advising him that unless the company was promptly filled and ready for muster, the order for raising it would be rescinded. North immediately mounted his pony and rode to Omaha, making the trip in a day and a half. He saw General Mitchell and explained the circumstances of the case, urging that in view of the time and money that he had expended further opportunity should be granted him. General Mitchell extended the time twenty days and Captain North returned to Columbus, enlisted thirty-five men, went to Fort Kearny and got fifty more, and got his brother, Luther, to enlist thirty-five more. This made more than one hundred, but when he reached Columbus he found that the thirty-five recruits whom he had left in the charge of Lieutenant Small, had all deserted because they had been told that they were being enlisted to go south to fight the negroes. However, by hard work and perseverance he secured enough men to make up the deficiency and on the thirteenth of January, 1865, he had his company mustered into the United States service by Captain Wilcox as Company A, Pawnee scouts. North was captain, Charles A. Small first lieutenant, and James Murie second lieutenant. The commissions of these officers were issued by Governor Saunders of Nebraska, October 24th, 1865.

The company was ordered into quarters at Columbus where they camped for a week, and then were sent on foot to Fort Kearny where they went into winter quarters. About the first of February arms were issued to them old style infantry muskets muzzle loaders, of course.

The commanding officer of the post, Captain Gillette of the First Nebraska cavalry, gave orders that the Pawnees should be thoroughly drilled in the manual of arms and this Captain North tried to do, for a time. The experiment, however, was a failure. The scouts did not understand the English tongue and in their language there were no words that would express the meaning of the orders to be given them. It was evident either that they must learn the English language or that words for their different commands used in the drill must be invented in their own tongue. Notwithstanding the explanation made to him, Captain Gillette insisted that the original orders must be obeyed. Captain North declared this was impossible, and urged besides that the Pawnees had been enlisted not as soldiers, but as scouts, spies and trailers and said that he would no longer attempt to teach them the manual of arms. Seeing that he could not make infantrymen of them, Captain Gillette, who seemed determined to keep them at work, ordered him to detail an officer and forty men and with ten days' rations to make a scout north to the Niobrara river and look for hostile Indians. The Pawnees had no horses and the order obliged them to set out on foot, though the snow was then ten or fifteen inches deep. Nevertheless, at daylight next morning, Lieutenant Small left the post with forty scouts, to cross the many channels of the half frozen Platte river, where in some places the scouts waded waist deep in the water. Notwithstanding the cold weather, no one complained. Upon reaching the Loup Fork, they encountered a severe snow storm, which obliged them to remain in camp for seven days, during which time the storm raged with fury. They ran out of provisions and were obliged to return to the post, the march being long and difficult for the weather was intensely cold, and many of the men had feet, hands and ears frozen.

At the post, the Pawnees were required to perform picket duty around the fort. The beats ran around it in a circle, and the sutlers' store was without this circle. The performance of this picket duty was amusing enough to outsiders, but not always so to those immediately concerned. The Pawnees could cry "Halt!" to a person, but could not say "Who goes there?" nor could they comprehend what was said to them. The man halted therefore, was in difficulties, for he could neither advance nor retreat. When halted in this manner, officers on their way to the sutlers' store were often obliged to shout at the top of their voices, calling for Captain North to come to their assistance, and to explain to the Pawnee sentry that the officer was free to pass. The commanding officer, after he himself had been caught in this trap, ordered that the Pawnees should abandon this service.

The Pawnee scouts were finally furnished with horses brought from Omaha, and were then ordered to march to Julesburg, which at that time was an important station on the Overland Stage road. On the way westward, they found frequent evidence of the hostility of the Sioux. At Plum creek they came upon one grave containing the bodies of fourteen men who had been killed by the Indians, while on their way to Pike's Peak. Emigrant wagons robbed of everything and dead oxen were constantly found along the way. In many cases, the wagons had been brought together and burned, so that nothing was found except the iron work. After a march of several days, the command reached the post of Fort Rankin-later Fort Sedgwick near Julesburg, and went into camp to await further orders.

Just before the arrival of the Pawnees at Julesburg, the Overland Stage station which was about one mile from the post, had been attacked and burned and several persons killed by the Cheyennes and Sioux. The post was garrisoned by Captain Nick O'Brien's company of the Seventh Iowa cavalry. The printed reports say that the Sioux and Cheyennes, some four or five hundred strong, had surprised the stage early in the day. Captain O'Brien with his company sallied out to drive them off, but the Indians not only held their ground but drove back the soldiers and almost surrounded them. The troops retreated to the post, which was threatened. The Indians then returned to the station, gathered up their plunder and retired to the bluff on the further side of the Platte river. Captain O'Brien's efforts to drive them away by shelling were unsuccessful, because of bad gunnery.

What had happened here from the Indian statements was this. The Sioux and Cheyennes had camped among the sand hills south of the Platte river at no great distance from Julesburg. They sent a party of seven warriors to ride up near to Fort Rankin in the hope that the troops would come out and pursue these few men into an ambuscade in the hills, where a large number of Indians were concealed.

The plan failed. Captain O'Brien pursued the group of Indians as expected, but before the troops reached the hills where they might have been surrounded, the Indians hidden there, showed themselves, and charged the troops and killed a number of them. Accounts differ as to the loss suffered by the troops, but the best report seems to show that fourteen soldiers and four citizens who were with them were killed. Some weeks later George Bent counted eighteen graves near the stockade about Fort Rankin.

At all events, the Indians attacked, captured and plundered the town of Julesburg and then left it.

It was during this summer that Luther North saw an example of endurance on the part of a Pawnee Indian. Luther had been sent to carry dispatches to North Bend, Nebraska, and as he rode out of Columbus, he overtook a Pawnee boy on foot. It was just noon and at the edge of town. The Pawnee boy asked where he was going and trotted along by his side. Luther was riding at a good jog trot. He inquired of the boy where he had come from and he said from the village of Genoa, which was twenty-two miles from Columbus. The boy ran alongside North's horse all the way to North Bend which was thirty-five miles from Columbus. They reached there at five, having made seven miles an hour for the whole distance. When North stopped at the stage station, the boy said "Are you going to stay here all night?" and then added "My father is camped on the river at Fremont" and went on. He was still running when last seen. Fremont was sixteen miles further on and so seventy-three miles from the Pawnee village. The boy had eaten nothing, and although the day was very hot, he had taken but one drink of water. At the crossing of Shell creek, where North had stopped to let his horse drink, the Indian had dipped up a couple of handfuls of water and put them on his head, and then drank a little, certainly not a glassful. This boy was not one of the Pawnee noted runners, but just an average boy. One of the great runners of the tribe once ran from the Pawnee agency in Oklahoma to the Wichita agency, one hundred and twenty miles in twenty-four hours and came back in twenty-four hours or less. This was over a rough, hilly, stony country.

CHAPTER VI

Early in the year, 1865, General Mitchell was relieved of his command of the district of Nebraska and General P. Edward Connor was appointed to succeed him. General Connor reached Julesburg from California, May 15th, bringing with him his staff and a portion of the Second California regiment. When he assumed command of the district, he announced that his headquarters would be in the field, and forthwith set about preparing for an expedition to the Powder river and Yellowstone country against the hostile Indians, Sioux and Cheyennes. He planned to have three separate columns march to a common objective point in that northern country.

One of these columns was to start from Omaha on the first day of June, under the command of Colonel Cole of the Second Missouri artillery. It was to consist of one battery of his own regiment and twelve companies of the Twelfth Missouri cavalry. They were to take ninety days' supplies. The route was to be from Omaha to Columbus, thence up the Loup river to its head, thence north, crossing the Niobrara, White Earth, Little Missouri and Powder rivers, to meet General Connor on the Yellowstone river on or about the first of September. Cole's new command made a great impression when it passed through Columbus. There were sixteen hundred men, all splendidly mounted and some artillery and it looked like a very effective force. However, as will be seen, it came very near being wiped out.

Another column under Colonel Walker of the Sixteenth Kansas cavalry, with six hundred men of his own regiment, several detachments of the Eleventh Ohio cavalry and other troops, in all about one thousand men, was to start from Fort Laramie on the fifth of June with fifty-five days rations. It was to proceed north, keeping east of the Black hills, crossing the Cheyenne river, and then the Little Missouri, about fifty miles south of where Colonel Cole was to cross, and to meet Colonel Cole at or near the mouth of the Tongue river on the first of September.

General Connor, with his staff and headquarters of the district, and detachments of the Seventh Iowa cavalry, Second California

46

cavalry, Pawnee scouts and a Signal corps under Lieutenants Brown and Richards, was to proceed from Julesburg to Fort Laramie and march direct to the mouth of the Tongue river where all three columns were to meet. The columns moved out substantially as arranged.

When General Connor reached Fort Laramie, then under command of General Stagg, he found that the volunteer troops there, who were to march with Colonel Walker, were greatly dissatisfied and more or less disorganized. They had been enlisted to serve for three years, or during the war of the Rebellion. Many were veterans who had re-enlisted for the war. At the close of the war, that spring, instead of being discharged and sent home, as they felt they should have been, they were ordered out on an Indian campaign. The result of this was that there were many desertions. When the order to march from Fort Laramie was read to them, the volunteers declared they would not obey. General Connor feared that the mutineers would fight and formed a line of battle of his own troops, together with the artillery. Just as the order for an attack was about to be given, the mutineers yielded and consented to go. They left Fort Laramie on the appointed day, under command of Colonel Walker. The direct distance between Fort Laramie and Tongue river was shorter than the routes to be followed by the other two columns and General Connor started from his camp on the Laramie river above Fort Laramie just about August first. At this point another company of Indian scouts, known as the Omaha scouts, had joined his command. Their officers were Captain Nash, First-lieutenant Evans and Second-lieutenant Mitchell, a brother of General Mitchell. These scouts were for the most part Winnebago Indians.

The command marched up the North Platte and crossed it, leaving the river near the point where Fort Fetterman afterwards stood. Thence they turned north to Brown Springs and the Cheyenne and Powder rivers, which they reached August 19th. Here they began the construction of a post, which was then called Camp Connor, and afterwards became known as Fort Reno. Captain North was required to furnish men from his company of scouts for picket duty, for

General Connor did not appear to feel much confidence in his Omaha scouts.

Three days after the command had reached this point, some of the Pawnee scouts came in to camp from the north and reported that they had discovered Indians. The whole company of Pawnee scouts was ordered out and started off in the hope of a big fight, having stripped off all their clothing, as was their custom when a battle was looked for. The trail when they reached it, showed that the Indians were traveling rapidly, that there were about forty head of horses and mules and that a travois was being dragged by one of them. This indicated a badly wounded man. The Pawnees followed the trail for fifteen miles, when it turned north for six or eight miles and then turning again, led back to Powder river, not far from the post. At dark, Captain North sent back to the camp with two of his lieutenants, the men who were riding the most tired horses, and with forty-eight of the best mounted Pawnees followed the retreating Indians, whose trail led down Powder river. When it grew so dark that it was no longer possible to see the trail from horseback, Captain North sent ahead two of his men on foot to follow it. They trotted forward all night long, constantly expecting to meet the Indians but being delayed at the frequent crossings of the river, where sometimes it took a long time to find out just where the Indians had left the water.

Just at daylight a little smoke was seen rising from a small grove of timber before them and when they came to the bank of the river they saw on the other side, a fire where the Indians had stopped to cook something to eat. They kept on as rapidly as possible, and presently, a few hundred yards ahead of them, discovered the retreating Indians, who saw their pursuers at about the same time. The Pawnees were riding in columns of twos, and from this the hostile Indians supposed that they were white troops. They stopped to fight, dismounted and spread out in a line of battle on the side of a small hill. The Pawnees rode steadily forward until they were within two hundred yards of the line of the enemy, when they began to shout their war cry and to slap their breasts. The discovery that these were Pawnees seemed to disconcert the enemy, who called to each other Panani, and forthwith broke and ran. The Pawnees killed seven at the first fire and later surrounding the ravine in which the hostiles had taken refuge, killed them all, twenty-six men and one woman.

At the beginning of the fight the animal attached to the travois became frightened and ran away and the wounded man on it rolled off, dragged himself to the edge of a nearby ravine and threw himself over the cut bank into it. He hoped to be overlooked and to escape. The Pawnees saw the act, and after killing the other Cheyennes returned for this man. The bank over which he had fallen was so high and steep that no one of the Pawnees was willing to clamber down after the man at the bottom, but a Pawnee sergeant with a sabre went around to the mouth of the ravine, followed it up and killed the wounded man. Among most Indian tribes there was seldom any taking of adult male prisoners. The loss of the Pawnees in the fight was only four horses.

These hostiles were a part of the Sioux and Cheyennes who had taken part in the Platte bridge fight, where Lieutenant Caspar Collins was killed. The Pawnees captured from them eighteen horses and seventeen mules, some of which bore government brands and had been taken from the soldiers in the Platte bridge fight These Indians had a number of white men's scalps, presumably those of soldiers killed at Platte bridge and also had articles of wearing apparel belonging to women and children, from which it was concluded that they had attacked and captured an emigrant train.

The success in this fight gave Frank North a tremendous reputation as a leader among his own people. The battle had taken but a short time, and before very long North started back with his party to the main camp. Their situation here was dangerous, for large camps of hostiles were believed to be in the immediate neighborhood and it was important as soon as possible to get back to some point where the horses of the Pawnees could rest.

Just at dark, Captain North rode into General Connor's camp, with his Pawnees carrying the scalps of the twenty-seven enemies and firing off their pistols and in other ways expressing their delight in their triumph. General Connor and his officers and in fact the whole

49

command, turned out to receive them and the troops formed a double line through which the Pawnees marched, singing their war songs, carrying the poles to which the scalps were attached and the captured arms, and driving before them the animals they had taken.

General Connor was greatly pleased at the success, praised Captain North and his men warmly, and issued an order complimenting the command which had won the first victory since the expedition had started out. The Pawnees, who had ridden one hundred and fifty miles without anything to eat, were now able to satisfy their hunger, but as soon as the meal was over, they asked General Connor's permission to celebrate their victory by a scalp dance. They danced about a great fire practically all night and around them stood the seven or eight hundred soldiers, who had gathered to witness the celebration.

The next morning, General Connor went to Captain North's quarters and directed him to have all the captured material brought out in front of the camp for his inspection. This was done and after looking the things over, General Connor said, "Captain North, you can again thank these men for me for their gallant conduct and success and you may distribute the property amongst them as you think best." Captain North thanked General Connor and distributed the plunder amongst those who had taken part in the fight, retaining for himself only a good horse.

The next night was devoted to further celebrations by the Pawnees, for then, according to the custom after a victorious battle, they changed their names. Such changes might be made only once during a campaign—during a particular warpath. It was after this fight that Captain North, whose Pawnee name hitherto had been White Wolf—Ski ri taka—was given a new name which the Pawnees asked him to choose himself. He preferred, however, that they should make the selection and they gave him the name Pani leshar the Pawnee chief a name said to have been given only once before to a white man, and then to General Fremont for whom they had a high regard.

On such an occasion the person receiving the new name was expected to present a gift to those naming him, and Captain North accordingly gave to the proper people the horse which he had chosen from among the animals captured in the recent fight.

General Connor moved the next day and Captain North sent with the Pawnee company wagon in the wagon train, as a guard, his orderly and two or three others of his men. During one of the halts of the train, a Pawnee guard who had been in the Sioux fight, while describing the battle to Captain North's orderly accidentally discharged his pistol and the ball struck the orderly in the forehead and killed him. The orderly was a Grand Pawnee while the other was Pawnee Loup, or Ski ri. The accident caused much feeling between the two bands and at one time it looked as if serious trouble might result, for the tribesmen of the orderly suspected that the killing was not accidental. However, Captain North investigated the matter that day and found that there was not and had not been, any apparent cause for difference between the two men, and since there appeared to have been no motive for the shooting, he decided it was an accident. The orderly was buried with military honors. After the funeral the leaders of the Pawnees made speeches to their people and declared that this accident was sent them by the Great Spirit to humiliate them for their glorification over the recent fight. They accepted this explanation.

CHAPTER VII

The next day, certain of the Pawnee scouts came into camp early and reported that they had discovered Indians. The whole company was ordered out and only a few miles from camp, Captain North saw from a high plateau three parties of Indians all traveling in the same direction, each party comprising forty or fifty people. He divided his command into three squads, sending one under Lieutenant Small to the right, another under Lieutenant Murie to the left, while he took the center squad. They then charged on the Indians who broke and ran, and a running fight followed for several miles. These were Cheyennes and because the Pawnee horses had not yet recovered from their recent long rides, the Pawnees could not overtake the enemy. Captain North, however, who had a fresh horse, was soon far in advance of the others, but could not get near enough to the Cheyennes to accomplish anything, though he fired several shots at them. The chase was kept up for some miles and when his men kept calling to him that their ponies were giving out, he ordered them to drop behind as their horses failed. Presently, however, having heard nothing for a little while, he looked back and saw that his men were a long way behind him, many of them going toward camp and on foot, leading their horses. North stopped, dismounted and fired at the nearest Cheyenne and then mounted and started to return. As he turned, about a dozen Indians came riding down upon him evidently intending to kill this man who was alone.

He rode as hard as he could, but the Indians soon overtook and passed him. Shots were fired at him and one of them hit his horse and disabled it. North dismounted and stood behind his horse as a breastwork. He fired a few shots and thus kept the Indians at a distance. Yet it seemed evident that they would soon close in on him, and he felt that he must make his way back to his men. He started running on foot, keeping the Indians off by pointing his rifle first at one and then at another, but before he had gone far, he discovered that he had left his two loaded revolvers behind him on the saddle, and ran back. He now tried to lead the horse with him with the purpose of using it as a protection against the Cheyenne bullets and arrows. It could walk and he kept on toward the camp for nearly a mile and presently saw, far off on a distant hill to the right, a man on horseback. Captain North waved to him, hoping that he would come to him and help, but the horseman presently turned and rode away out of sight.

North was short of ammunition and felt pretty sure that the Cheyennes would finally get him, but he kept them off by pointing his rifle at them. After he had gone a little further, he saw Lieutenant Small ride over a little hill toward him, not more than half a mile away. Lieutenant Small had left his squad of troops and had ridden up on a hill to look about and when he saw Captain North, he charged down toward him. The Cheyennes turned and retreated, no doubt believing that the scouts were following and would soon appear over the hill.

The two men went on back together, taking turns in riding the unwounded horse. Presently as they went over a ridge they saw down in the valley of a little branch of Powder river, a number of Indians who had apparently surrounded someone that they were trying to capture. A little examination of the group seemed to show that they were Pawnees and the two men approached them, keeping out of sight until both could hear the voices of the Indians, when they found that they were Pawnees. They had corralled an old Cheyenne who had been cut off from his party and had been shooting at him until he was wounded in many places. He on his part was holding them off with his bow and arrows. Captain North and Lieutenant Small came up with the party and the captain ordered them to stop shooting at the Cheyenne and to kill him at once. A Pawnee ran up to the logs behind which the Cheyenne was lying and struck at him with the sabre, wounding him in the left hand and at the same time seized his bow and jerked it away from the Cheyenne, who with his butcher knife in his hand sprang from behind the log pile and made a rush, hoping to get through the line of Pawnees, but a dozen bullets pierced him and he fell dead. He was at once struck and scalped by the Pawnees. The dead man was identified by Nick Janice who was with the Pawnees, as Red Bull, a Cheyenne.

There still were many Cheyennes in the neighborhood, but because of the condition of the Pawnee horses, Captain North saw that no fighting with them could be had. Accordingly, he sent a message to General Connor telling him about his horses and asking for reinforcements. General Connor ordered Colonel Kidd with six companies of the Sixth Michigan cavalry to march to North's support, and notified North of the order. Meantime, efforts were made to get in close touch with the Cheyennes, but since they had plenty of good horses, they would retreat whenever the Pawnees advanced toward them and when the Pawnees went back to their position, the Cheyennes would follow them up. After a time Colonel Kidd came up with his command. He had a fine regiment which had belonged to the Sixth Army corps in the Civil war, but these were some of the men who felt that they should have been discharged at the end of the Rebellion, and now did not feel like fighting Indians. They believed that their officers were to blame for their being compelled to remain in the service, and had threatened to shoot Colonel Kidd and other officers.

Captain North knew of this feeling on the part of the men, and wished if possible to relieve Colonel Kidd of a possible danger, yet at the same time to get into a fight with the Cheyennes.

He said to him, Colonel, if you will give me a fresh mount of horses for my men, I will go back and fight those Cheyennes but I cannot do anything with my played-out horses.

I cannot do that, replied the colonel, because the men are so attached to their horses that they would be unwilling to let anyone else have them.

Well then, said Captain North, I'll send some of my best men with you to show you where the Indians are, so that you can fight them.

To this Colonel Kidd agreed, and North detailed Lieutenant Murie with a few of his best mounted men to go with Colonel Kidd's command, while he himself returned to camp with the remaining Pawnees and reported to General Connor what had happened.

After Colonel Kidd had gone a short distance toward where the Indians were supposed to be, he sent Lieutenant Murie with his

Pawnees and one of his own officers to go ahead and from the top of a hill to learn if possible the exact location of the Indians. They were to return and report as soon as possible.

These instructions were followed, and from the top of the hill Murie discovered the Cheyennes concentrated in a little flat beyond, ready and waiting for a fight. It was now nearly dusk and Murie and his men hastened back to the main command. Suddenly, at a distance in the direction of the main camp, was seen a cloud of dust and when he reached the place where he expected to report to Colonel Kidd, the command had disappeared. It was presently obvious that the dust seen was raised by Colonel Kidd and his troops, who were riding back to camp at a gallop. Murie and his scouts did not understand what had happened and returned to camp, riding slowly all the way. Murie reported to Captain North, who directed him to report in person to General Connor, which he did that night. The general listened with interest and appeared surprised, but said nothing beyond asking a few questions.

Early next morning General Connor sent word to all his captains to report to him at once and they soon appeared at headquarters. General Connor mounted his horse and ordered them to follow him as he rode down to Camp Connor, two miles distant, where Colonel Kidd and his regiment were building the post. When they reached the camp, Colonel Kidd was called from his quarters and there in the hearing of the officers, General Connor in a quiet and polite manner, proceeded to reprimand him for his abandonment of Lieutenant Murie. He told him that he was not fit to command troops or be in the army in any capacity and that under any other circumstances he would have court-martialed him for cowardice, but that this was impossible at the time, as the command had been ordered out for the Tongue river campaign and was already on the move. When General Connor had expressed these views, he said quietly "That is all" and then with his officers turned and left Colonel Kidd without saying good-by.

General Connor's purpose in having his captains present on the occasion of the reprimand was no doubt to humiliate Colonel Kidd as much as possible and at the same time to suggest to the officers the disgrace that anyone might expect to follow similar conduct. Connor and his officers now joined the command which had moved on down Tongue river.

CHAPTER VIII

After marching for five days, the command struck a heavy Indian trail going west, which, however, was two or three weeks old. It had been made by a large party of Indians. General Connor wished to follow this trail, but before doing so, he desired to learn more about it. He therefore sent Captain North with ten Pawnees to follow the trail, telling him that the main command would follow the stream he was on down to Tongue river and wait there for a report from the scouts. Captain North with his ten men followed the trail for about twenty-five miles, and about noon he noticed that one of his men had dropped behind and was earnestly looking ahead as if he saw something. Presently, the scout signaled to the captain to come back to him and the scout pointed out some distant objects, which looked like buffalo. North examined them with his field glasses and declared that they were buffalo. He handed the glasses to the scout, telling him to look and give his opinion. The man looked through the glasses and said they were horses and Indians.

North resumed the advance, following the trail down through a ravine into the valley of Tongue river and presently, without being discovered, they worked themselves to a point where they could see the Indian camp. They were still too far away to count the number of lodges or to estimate the size of the camp and North ordered two of his Pawnees to approach as near as possible to the village and learn the number of lodges and something definite as to the character of the camp. The two Pawnees stripped themselves and by following down the creek and creeping under the stream banks, they came close to the village. They were so near to a woman who came down to the stream for water that they could almost have touched her. In less than an hour, they returned to Captain North and reported that it was a large camp.

North wrote to General Connor a note telling him what had been learned and requesting him to send forward all the Pawnees and one company of cavalry with which to attack the camp. Two of the Pawnees were detailed to carry this note to General Connor and they were ordered to make the best time they could, even if they killed their horses.

North and his eight men kept themselves hidden in the brush all that day and closely watched the Indians. The position was one of some danger. The neighing of a horse or the wandering about of some occupant of the camp might have led to their discovery at any moment. When darkness set in, they quietly moved away from their position to a safer location, six miles further off. During the night Captain North posted pickets on both sides of the river to keep a sharp lookout for the troops he had sent for. He and his men remained awake all night, holding their horses in readiness for instant action if necessary. Just at dawn some Pawnees were seen approaching, and were hailed by North. They told him that General Connor himself was on the way, with four hundred men and two pieces of artillery. The message had been delayed because, in order to get better grass for the horses, General Connor had moved down Tongue river twenty-five miles further than he had at first intended. This made the distance fifty miles further for the messengers to ride and the troops to march. The troops had just gone into camp when the messengers reached them. The general asked the Pawnee riders as to the size of the Indian village, and they replied that they did not know exactly, but told him by signs that there were many horses.

General Connor at once decided to go in person and to take with him about four times the number of troops asked for by Captain North. This proved most fortunate. Had he not done so, the warriors of this large village might have completely annihilated the small force that Captain North had sent for. The Pawnees afterwards declared that this was another proof that the Great Spirit was watching Captain North with a protecting eye.

Soon after the return of the messengers, General Connor appeared with his command and when joined by Captain North at once asked, as if anxious to attack the Indians without delay, How far is the village from here? About six miles was the reply. Show us the way, captain, and let us push on, said the general, notwithstanding the troops had marched seventy-five miles since they had had any rest.

North at once went on with his scouts, leading the way along the bottom, through the willows and in the river bed. He took the command to a point within three-quarters of a mile of the Indian village before they were discovered. They were then obliged to move out on the open plain. As stated in The Fighting Cheyennes? the Indians had been warned of the approach of the troops, but did not credit the informant.

Their unexpected appearance caused great commotion in the Indian camp. The Indians rushed for their horses and General Connor immediately ordered a charge. The next moment the troops went galloping into the Indian village, spreading consternation there. The Indians left their lodges and fled in every direction. The troops followed the men for fifteen miles into the Big Horn mountains, and killed one hundred and sixty-two of them.® Besides these, a number of women and children were killed by the Pawnee, Omaha and Winnebago scouts, notwithstanding the strict orders of General Connor that no women or children were to be killed. The Indian scouts did this work at times when they were not observed by the soldiers. It was afterwards learned that the camp consisted of two hundred and fifty lodges, or about fifteen hundred persons, of whom five hundred were warriors, the whole village being under command of Old Black Bear, a noted Arapaho chief.

The village was a very rich one. The plunder was so tempting that, while the running fight of the morning was going on, many of the Pawnees and a number of the white soldiers dropped back and commenced to gather up spoils and to hunt for straggling women and children in the brush. General Connor was indignant at this and punished the men for their misconduct

About one o'clock in the afternoon the soldiers returned to the village, and many of the Arapahoes gathered together, followed them back, and stationed themselves in the timber on the opposite bank of the river, near the village, with a view to picking off the men while they were engaged in destroying the lodges and collecting plunder. General Connor accordingly brought the artillery into service and from a slight elevation, overlooking the village, he shelled the Indians in the timber, so that they were forced to withdraw. Nevertheless, they continued to annoy the troops considerably by circling around the camp and every now and then making a dash within gun-shot and firing a volley.

The whole command now having been concentrated, the work of burning the village was begun and in the course of an hour was completed. The scouts then rounded up all the horses and mules and when they were counted, it was found that there were seven hundred and fifty captured animals. Some of the animals were loaded with plunder, and between two and three o'clock the command started on the return march to the wagon train. All were greatly elated with the victory, which had been won with the loss of but one man a Winnebago scout. There were thirteen wounded, of whom one—a sergeant of the signal corps afterwards died. The enemy lost more than one hundred and sixty warriors killed, as well as a number of women and children, and seventeen women were taken prisoners.

On the return to the village, during its destruction and on the march away from it, the hostiles were very bold and defiant. They were provided with horses that were fresh, strong and swift and were able to dash up close to the troops who, because their horses were exhausted, could not pursue them. Captain North often spoke of the marvellous exhibitions of riding that he saw that day.

The command reached the wagon train on Tongue river about two o'clock in the morning, having traveled fifty miles in about twelve hours, without rest or food. At about ten o'clock in the morning, General Connor issued an order that the troops engaged in the fight should bring out all their plunder and pile it up in front of their respective company quarters. The order was promptly obeyed and an immense quantity of plunder was thus brought together.

In their pile the Pawnees included about sixty scalps which they had taken in the fight. The men supposed that General Connor intended, as on a previous occasion, to have everything distributed among the victors, but this was not at all in his thought. The men were greatly astonished and mortified, therefore, when, after they had been drawn up in line, General Connor addressed them in terms of the severest condemnation for their conduct in having to a great extent abandoned the fight, in order to plunder the village. He gave them a terrible scoring, explaining, however, that his remarks were intended only for those who deserved the reprimand. He concluded by saying, "To punish you for this unsoldierlike conduct, I propose to destroy everything that you have taken."

He at once ordered a guard of twelve soldiers, whom he selected for the purpose, to set fire to the various piles of captured material, and in half an hour it was all destroyed. Among the articles thus burned up, were a fine lot of native implements and a large number of buffalo robes. General Connor's rebukes were sweeping and savage but he made a few exceptions in favor of the Pawnees and some of the white soldiers. When the flames had subsided, he passed along the line of the Pawnees and selecting those who had done gallant service in the fight he told them to go to the bunch of captured horses, which were confined in the corral, and pick out the best ones for themselves, each Pawnee to take only one horse.

General Connor now sent for the women prisoners, and when they were brought out he succeeded in finding some of them who could speak the Sioux language and through Nick Janice, the Sioux interpreter, they said that they were Arapahoes, and gave a detailed statement concerning their band.

General Connor then said to them, "I am going to send you back to your people. I will allow you to pick out horses for yourselves, and will give you some tobacco which I want you to present to Black Bear as a peace offering and tell him that if, within the next thirty days, he will return to Fort Laramie with his people, we will not molest them, but, if he does not do this, at the end of thirty days we will take up the trail and will kill them all."

The women went to the corral and picked out the horses which had belonged to their families and, upon being supplied with a few days' rations, they left the camp and took the trail up Tongue river to join their people. They took with them letters from General Connor to the commanding officer at Fort Laramie asking him to receive the Arapahoes and hold them until his return to that post.

CHAPTER IX

A day or two after the capture of the Arapaho village, General Connor led his command down Tongue river to its junction with the Yellowstone, the march occupying ten days. He reached that point about the first of September, this being the time and place set for meeting the commands of Colonel Cole and Colonel Walker. Here General Connor's command went into camp, and the country was scouted to the westward through the Panther mountains, while other scouts were sent southward to look for the two commands. As several days passed without news of Colonel Cole's command, General Connor became uneasy about them, for he feared they might be out of rations. He ordered Captain North to take fifty of his Pawnees and proceed to Powder river to search for traces of Colonel Cole.

Accordingly, on the morning of the eighth of September, Captain North started out with his Pawnees through a heavy rainstorm. The men took only the small quantity of provisions which they could carry on their own horses and expected to live on the game they could kill. All day long they rode through a drenching rain and after traveling thirty-five miles, went into camp in a cañon in the mountains.

During the night the rain turned into sleet, and this continued all the next day. On the open plain next morning the storm was so severe and blinding that it was impossible for North to keep his course. The men had never been in that part of the country and they had no guides. They traveled about ten miles by a small pocket compass and, the storm increasing, they were obliged to camp and to remain there the rest of the day and all night. Next morning the sun came out bright and warm, the command resumed its march and by noon the sleet had entirely disappeared.

During the day they killed some buffalo and secured enough meat, as they thought, to last them for the trip. They discovered frequent signs of Indians and at about three o'clock in the afternoon two scouts who had been sent on ahead returned and reported that they had sighted a big Indian village, on Powder river.

Captain North thereupon moved off to the right, finally leading his force into a deep timbered cañon of the mountains, where it would be hidden. With three of his best men he then climbed to a high point on the mountain whence he could overlook the Powder river valley. With his glasses he could see Indians moving about and smoke rising from a camp in the timber, but from his position could draw no conclusions as to its size.

After dark Captain North and his people went down to the river below the Indian camp, which was on the west side of the stream. They had found no traces of the troops for whom they were looking. Two men were sent across the river to look about, and when they returned a few hours later, they reported having found Colonel Cole's trail, which seemed only two or three days old. Captain North at once crossed the river and followed the trail up the stream for about half a mile. Near here, on the west side of the river, Captain North found where Colonel Cole had camped during the storm. The ground was literally strewn with dead horses; nine hundred were counted. The men were overcome with astonishment and wonder at this sight, for they did not know how the animals had come to their death. Many of the horses had been shot through the head and at first North thought that a terrible fight had taken place between the troops and the Indians and that the troops had killed their horses and used them as breast-works. Yet places were found where fires had been built, in which bridles and saddles and other equipment had been burned. Iron bits and rings, stirrups, buckles and other metal parts of horse furniture were found in the ashes.

Under the impression that a terrible fight had taken place, Captain North felt that it was not safe for him to remain there with a force of only fifty men, and he accordingly resumed the trail, which led up the Powder river to a point from which the Indian camp, which had been discovered the day before, could be plainly seen. The trail seemed to lead straight into this camp. Night was approaching, and Captain North at once set out to return to General Connor's camp on Tongue river. Riding all night and the next day, he arrived at the camp just at dark, having made in twenty-four hours, the ride which had occupied almost three days on their outward scout. Captain

North at once reported to General Connor, who was equally at a loss, to reach any satisfactory conclusion concerning the deserted camp and the dead horses.

Early next morning the general with his whole command moved out of camp, following the old trail up Tongue river to reach Colonel Cole's command. For five days forced marches were made up the river. It was evident that the general was much worried concerning the safety of Colonel Cole, whose men he knew must be suffering for food.

On the fifth day out from camp, after the horses had been unsaddled, General Connor went to Captain North and said, I can't endure this terrible uncertainty any longer. I must find Cole's command as soon as possible. I want you to take forty or fifty of your scouts, as you may see fit and with ten days rations on pack mules, go across the country from this point and try to head off Cole and give his men temporary relief.

Very well, general, I'll start at once, replied the captain.

Here is a letter of instructions to Colonel Cole, said the general as he handed it to him. When you reach Tongue river, if you find the trail only two days old send back to me five men with the information. If the trail is over two days old then send five men ahead, on the trail, with the letter of instructions and you return to camp. I will remain here until I hear from you.

North set out at once. The command rode until midnight, rested until daylight, and then resumed the march. Early in the afternoon they reached Powder river and in the valley struck Colonel Cole's trail, which looked to be less than two days old. Captain North thereupon wrote a note to that effect to General Connor, stating also that he would overtake Colonel

Cole and bring his command to the crossing of Clear creek. After sending off the five couriers with this note, he pushed forward on the trail and by ten o'clock at night had ridden fifty miles further. On the way he passed two of Cole's camps which showed that the trail was older than at first supposed, for if it was only two days old he should have overtaken him by this time. Every now and then horses, dead from starvation and exhaustion, were found on the trail and told a pitiful tale of suffering. Next morning at daylight, the scouts pushed on.

At two o'clock in the afternoon North sighted Cole's column moving up the Powder river. This was on the nineteenth of September, just nineteen days after the expiration of the time for which the command had been supplied with rations. Captain North and his men rode up to the command on a full gallop, their sudden appearance creating an indescribable commotion and excitement among the famished and disheartened soldiers, who cheered with enthusiasm and threw up their hats for joy. It was a large body of men, for Colonel Walker had joined Colonel Cole at the appointed place of meeting on Powder river, during the latter part of August. Colonel Cole being the senior officer had taken command of the whole force.

The men were actually in a starving condition. Thirty-five had died from starvation and exposure and all seemed thin and emaciated, their horses looking even worse. Many of the animals had died from starvation and the remainder were mere skeletons. There were only six hundred left, and these because of their weak- ness could not be used. Twelve hundred cavalrymen had thus been reduced to footmen. The men obliged to travel on foot had become lame and footsore and had wrapped their feet in saddle blankets and gunny sacks. It was only with pain and great difficulty that they could walk at all.

The starving men flocked around Captain North and his command to get something to eat and seeing that the Pawnees had some supplies they offered as high as five dollars each for a piece of hard-tack. They had recently been paid off and had plenty of money, which they offered the Pawnees in exchange for food. Captain North, however, ordered the Pawnees not to take any money, but to distribute the crackers among the soldiers, giving two crackers to each man. There are thirteen in a ration, and the three hundred rations, therefore, contained three thousand and nine hundred crackers. Beans, bacon, coffee and sugar were distributed in like manner, each man receiving about one-sixth of a full ration.

As soon as the distribution was completed Captain North reported in person to Colonel Cole, who had not the least idea of the country nor of where he was going. He knew from his maps, that if he followed up Powder river, he would be within easy march of the North Platte river. Knowing that troops were stationed on that stream, he hoped to reach them before his force was completely prostrated by starvation. When Captain North informed him that he was not far from supplies, he wept with joy. The captain also told him that he had ordered the rations of the Pawnees to be distributed among the soldiers as the Pawnees needed nothing to eat. The captain knew just where the command was and that camp Connor was only about twenty-five miles distant. On the day before he overtook Colonel Cole, he had passed the place where the Pawnees had killed the twenty-seven Cheyenne Indians. The Pawnees had called his attention to the spot. They had pointed out to him where the different Indians had been killed and the ravine where the wounded warrior had been dispatched with a sabre.

Colonel Cole at once ordered a commissioned officer, with a detachment of his best mounted troops and four mule teams, to set out that afternoon and make all possible haste to camp Connor, with a requisition for supplies. The officer was to return at once and meet the command, which would move up the river.

That evening Captain North asked Colonel Cole to explain the mystery of the dead horses, It is quite a story, said the colonel, and when I tell it to you, you will see that we have had a terrible experience for the last two or three weeks. On the eighth day of September, we started out from Tongue river in a fearful rainstorm and were attacked by Red Cloud himself with twenty-five hundred warriors. He was anxious to stop our march up the Powder river for his whole camp, men, women and children, numbering some nine or ten thousand persons in all was located on the stream and if we kept on we were bound to strike it. During this rainstorm the cavalrymen were in their saddles all day long fighting these twenty-five hundred warriors. There was no cessation of hostilities until night came, when we returned to our camp, which was located on the open plain on the west bank of the river, as you observed. Our front was formed with fourteen companies of cavalry and some artillery, and the wagon train was located at one end of the camp. The horses formed the line of defense, within which the soldiers were stationed, thus being protected inside of the hollow square. The animals were tied by their halters to the picket line. They had been worked so hard during the day that they had become tired and overheated, and when the rain turned into sleet and snow it chilled them, and many of them died. Many of the horses were found next morning standing up, so benumbed and stiff that they could not move one foot in front of the other and we had to shoot them.

That explains the mystery, said Captain North, which so puzzled the Pawnees and me. You burned the equipment to keep it from falling into the hands of the Indians.

Yes, we could not carry those things with us.

Colonel, why didn't you go into the large grove of timber just below your camp? It seems to me that would have afforded you protection both from the Indians and the storm. I was out in the storm and my men had ridden their horses very hard, but when the rain changed into sleet I sought protection in a ravine, said the captain.

I could not get into the timber as the Indians held it from me, replied the colonel.

Captain North did not press his inquiries further, but he thought it strange that Colonel Cole had not made a fight to reach the timber, even though it was held by the Indians.

The next morning Colonel Cole moved his command and marched to a point within six miles of camp Connor, where they met the supply train. His troops had been twenty-one days without anything to eat except the meat of starved horses and they had nearly given up hope when Captain North came to their relief with the small supply of food which the Pawnees carried.

Captain North hid overtaken Colonel Cole about forty miles above Clear creek, wither General Connor had ordered the captain to lead the Cole command. Captain North detailed ten Pawnees to go to

Clear creek, and there await the arrival of General Connor and notify him of Cole's arrival at camp Connor. The detail reached the crossing at the same time with General Connor, the general having made a forced march up Tongue river. General Connor had with him two hundred and fifty wagons, loaded with supplies sufficient to last the whole united command for a sixty days' campaign. He at once took up his march for camp Connor, the journey occupying two days.

Captain North knew that the demoralized condition of Cole's command would frustrate all General Connor's former plans. He wished to learn what the general intended to do and as General Connor was approaching the camp, North rode out some miles and met him. Captain North gave him a graphic description of the condition of Cole's command and told him of the great number of Indians which Cole said he had encountered during his march up the Powder river.

General Connor was surprised at the information and the general condition of affairs.

What do you propose to do now, general? asked the captain.

I am going to give these troops two weeks rest and then organize the dismounted men as a regiment of infantry and take the whole command down Powder river and clean out those Indians, replied the general.

Upon reaching camp Connor, however, the plans of the general were frustrated. A mail from Fort Laramie had arrived and the very first document handed to General Connor was an order relieving him from the command of the district of the plains and directing him to turn over his district to General Frank Wheaton, a regular army officer. On starting out on this campaign the war of the Rebellion being over and volunteer troops being mustered out every day General Connor had feared that when he got well into the Indian country and had his plans arranged for a successful campaign, orders to relieve him might come just at the time when his efforts might be on the point of being successful. He, therefore, left strict orders with his adjutant-general to retain all official mail for him at that post until his return. Yet the very paper which General Connor had taken such pains to avoid receiving had now come. General Connor was much chagrined at the order. He considered his campaign a failure thus far and was reluctant to abandon it without further effort. There was nothing for him to do, however, but to obey, and he at once ordered his troops to prepare for the march to Fort Laramie, where General Wheaton was waiting. With some of his officers, he went on ahead in ambulances and reached Fort Laramie the first week in October.

The general turned over the command of the district to General Wheaton and then proceeded to Camp Douglas, at Salt Lake, whence he was ordered to Washington. There he was promoted to the rank of major-general of Volunteers and was mustered out of the service. His troops reached Fort Laramie about ten days after his departure and the volunteers were ordered to their respective states to be mustered out.

Colonel Cole, with his command, went to Saint Louis. Later, he was court-martialed for lack of judgment in not going into the grove of timber on the Powder river during the storm in which he lost so many horses. The court decided, on account of his good record, to acquit him with a reprimand.

The time of enlistment of the Pawnees expired on the fifteenth day of October and General Wheaton informed Captain North that he was prepared either to muster the scouts out of the service, or to order them to relieve a company of the Seventh cavalry at the Pawnee reservation, where the captain should have command of the post during the winter. The captain accepted the latter proposition, as the Pawnees would thus be at home with their people and yet would draw pay and rations. He accordingly started with them for the reservation, six hundred miles away, and arrived there safely.

CHAPTER X

In January, 1866, Captain North received orders to send fifty of his men to Fort Kearny to join a scouting party that was to go south and west from there, along the Republican river. He detailed Lieutenant Murie to go and when Luther North asked permission to accompany the scouts, his brother assented. This was Luther's first trip with the Pawnee scouts. He had no command.

They marched to Fort Kearny and joined the scouting party which consisted of two troops of cavalry, besides the fifty Pawnee scouts. They went southwest from Kearny to the Republican and up that river to the Frenchman's Fork, twenty miles beyond. Here they made a permanent camp from which scouting parties were sent out. Murie usually went with the scouts. The country was full of elk, deer and wild turkeys and there were some buffalo. One morning the commanding officer sent word to Murie to send ten men south fifteen or twenty miles to see what they could find. Luther North went with them. They rode south until the middle of the afternoon, when off to the southwest they saw a band of Indians. These had seen the scouts and were coming toward them on the run. There seemed to be about one hundred and fifty of them. Luther told the scouts to run back to a nearby creek where they could get under the bank and fight there. The Pawnees were armed with Spencer carbines. As the Indians were mostly armed with bows and arrows and the weather was very cold, it did not seem probable that they would fight long. The scouts were well mounted and started back on a gallop, but did not try to hurry their horses. The Indians gained on them.

When they were within perhaps half a mile of the creek, Luther's horse slipped on some ice and fell and Luther struck his head on the frozen ground and was knocked unconscious. When he regained his senses, one of the scouts had his head in his lap and was rubbing his face with snow. The scouts had all dismounted when Luther's horse fell and had formed a circle around him and were fighting the Indians off. At first, the Indians had charged up pretty close, but the repeating guns were new to them and they broke and circled around.

Five of the scouts' horses were wounded with arrows. That made them hard to handle.

This showed the scouts' great bravery and loyalty, for there were at least one hundred hostile Indians in the band. The scouts were well mounted and could easily have outrun them if they had left the white man, but they never thought of that. When Luther was able to sit up, the man that was caring for him helped him on his horse and they started for the creek. The Indians charged them, but when they stopped and faced about, the Indians also stopped. Some of them got between the scouts and the creek and even into the creek bed, but they scattered and got out of the way as the scouts approached them. The Indians made two or three charges, but never came very close. About sundown they rode off toward the south. Three of the scouts' horses were so badly wounded that they could not live and had to be killed. The scouts turned back toward the camp, which they reached after midnight and reported what had taken place.

The next morning, about the time the command was ready to start in pursuit of the Indians, a courier came in from Fort Kearny, ordering the whole command back to the fort. This ended that campaign. Soon after reaching Fort Kearny, the scouts were ordered back to the Pawnee agency, where they were mustered out the following April, 1866.

That summer an incident took place near Columbus which showed the regard in which the Pawnees held Frank North and their confidence in him.

Frank and Luther North were engaged in putting up hay, when one day at noon, as they were lying under the shade of the wagon, they were surprised to see the chiefs of the Pawnee tribe ride into the field and dismount near them. They were a fine looking group of men. The visit came about in this way:

While the Pawnees were on their buffalo hunt that summer, the Ski-ri band for some reason got separated from the other three bands and had no luck in killing buffalo. The Tsau i, Pita hau i rat and Kit ka hahki, on the other hand, had very good luck and killed so many buffalo that they cached a lot of dried meat on the Little

Blue river. The Ski ri found the cache and broke it open, taking some of the meat. Later they found buffalo and made a good killing before they came home. The other three bands were the first to get home from their hunt and when the Ski ri band came, they camped on the south side of the Loup river. La tah cots le shar, Eagle Chief, head chief of the Ski ri band, crossed the river and going to the lodge of Pita le shar u, Chief Man, head chief of the Pawnees, told him about the taking of the meat and asked him to call a council of all the chiefs, to decide what the Ski ri band should pay for the meat. The council was called, but the men could not agree. After some pretty fiery speeches had been made and threats had been made that they would declare war, Ska ta la le shar, Lone Chief, a Ski ri, proposed that they all go down to see Pani le shar, chief of the Pawnees.

There were sixteen chiefs in the Pawnee tribe, four for each band and these were the men who came to the hayfield. After shaking hands with the two brothers, they sat down in a circle, filled the pipe and after smoking told their story. Ti ra wat le shar, Spirit Chief, who was the greatest orator in the Pawnee tribe, made a speech praising Frank North as a great warrior and a man of wisdom, and wound up by telling the trouble they were having and asking him to decide how much the Ski ri should pay. They had all agreed that his decision should be final. Frank North answered his speech and appointed a committee of four of the chiefs, one from each band, to find out how much meat the Ski ri had taken. They were to return the same amount of meat to the families owning the cache. The chiefs he chose were Kuruks ta puk, Fighting Bear, Ti ra wat le shar, Spirit Chief, Ska ta la le shar, Lone Chief and the other Pita le shar, Chief Man. No one questioned his decision. They all said "Lau, lau" and went home satisfied.

Ska-dik, Crooked Hand, the greatest warrior in the tribe and a Ski ri, who had been against paying anything for the meat that was taken, said, "Well if our father says that is right, it is right and we will pay." This man, Crooked Hand, was the greatest warrior in the Pawnee tribe. It was said that he had killed more than one hundred of the enemies of the Pawnees. He was a good friend of the whites. In one of the Pawnee battles with the Sioux near Genoa, he killed six

Sioux warriors, and at the scalp dance after the fight, he wore a robe made from the hide of a black and white steer, and fastened around the border of the robe were seventy-one scalps that he had taken. He was a medium-sized man, quick in action and speech and also quick tempered, but good natured and always full of fun. He told Luther North this story about one of his adventures.

The Pawnees and the Yankton Sioux had made a treaty of peace and had visited back and forth and Crooked Hand had gone to visit the chief of the Yank-tons. While he was there, a Yankton who had been out with a hunting party, came home with a report that while hunting on the Cedar river, they had been attacked by a Pawnee war-party and all except himself had been killed. The Yanktons were very much excited over the news and a lot of the young warriors went to the lodge of the chief where Crooked Hand was visiting. Crowding into the lodge, they said they were going to kill Crooked Hand. The chief stood in front of Crooked Hand and tried to reason with them, but they insisted on killing him. He did not understand the Sioux language, but knew they were after him.

So he stepped out from behind the chief and commenced talking in sign language. He told them he had come as a friend and had done nothing to make them angry, but that he was not afraid; he had fought Yank-tons many times; that he was full of Yankton blood up to his neck and that if they wanted him now, to come and get him. When he got this far with his story, he laughed and said, "Oh, my father, I talked very brave, but down here (and he pointed to his heart) I was jumping up and down." Well, the young Yanktons did not get him and that night the chief took him across the Missouri river, gave him two good horses and told him to ride. Three or four days later he reached home.

A few days after that a war-party of Yanktons came down to the Pawnee village and, surprising a lot of Pawnee women in the cornfield, killed a number of them. In the fight that followed the Pawnees killed a great warrior and medicine-man of the Yankton tribe. He was killed by the government interpreter, Baptiste Behale and the Pawnees had a great scalp dance over it.

CHAPTER XI

On the first day of March, 1867, General Augur, then commanding the department of the Platte, telegraphed to Captain North, at the Pawnee agency, to come at once to Omaha. When he reached there General Augur welcomed him cordially and said:

Captain, you have done good work on the frontier with your Pawnees and have made them a valuable branch of our frontier army. I have sent for you to request you to enlist two hundred Pawnee scouts as soon as possible for some frontier service which they can perform better than anybody else. I want you to organize them into two companies of cavalry. What do you think of it?

General, I think I can do so, but that will only give me a captain's commission, said North. I feel as if I deserve something better, for I have already served as captain.

You are right, said the general, What do you think you ought to have?

Captain North made this suggestion: I will organize two hundred scouts into a battalion of four companies to be known as the first battalion of the Pawnee scouts. This ought to give me a major's commission and I will ask for only one captain and one lieutenant for each company and the regular number of non-commissioned officers. By this arrangement, general, I can be given a major's commission without increasing the expense of the service.

Your proposition strikes me favorably, said General Augur, and you deserve a major's commission. Go and organize the battalion of scouts as you have suggested and you shall have it.

General, I will at once go ahead with the work. By the way, what service are we to perform and in what part of the country?

You are not wanted for any regular Indian campaign, but for duty along the line of the Union Pacific railroad. The Indians are troubling the construction gangs killing the workmen and running off the horses every day. This must be stopped and as soon as possible.

Very well, I'll have the battalion in the field in a few days, replied Major North. He said good-by to the general and set out for the reservation.

When he told the Pawnees of his mission, they were enthusiastic over the prospect. He had no trouble in enlisting the two hundred men and by the fifteenth of March they were thoroughly organized and had been brought down to the Union Pacific railroad. It was a fine command and Major North felt proud of it. The Pawnees were taken by rail to old Fort Kearny, to remain there until they received their horses. Major North and Colonel Merrill, inspector-general of the department, were ordered to inspect, and purchase the horses.

The four company battalion was made up of:

COMPANY A-Captain, E. W. Arnold, First-lieutenant, Isaac Davis.

Company B Captain, James Murie, First-lieutenant, Fred Matthews.

Company C Captain, Charles E. Morse, First-lieu-tenant, William Rudy.

Company D Captain, Luther H. North, First-lieu-tenant, Gus G. Becher.

The Pawnees remained at Fort Kearny for a month, and then, when they had received their horses, Major North marched them to O'Fallon's bluffs. There they crossed the North Platte river and went on to the end of the railroad track, which was about where Alkali station is now located. Two companies were immediately sent on to Julesburg (Fort Sedgwick), sixty miles distant, to exchange the old muzzle loading weapons, which had been supplied them, for Spencer carbines.

The Indians had been greatly annoying the graders and track-layers by shooting at them and by running off the horses and mules. Two or three days before the arrival of Major North a large number of horses had been taken from the contractors. Major North, accordingly, with the two remaining companies, moved along with the workmen, who were building the road at the rate of two miles a day. On the second day after Major North's arrival his pickets came in and reported that a party of Indians were coming down from the north. He at once took a detachment of forty men under Luther North and Captain Morse and by making a circuit got between the North Platte river and the approaching Indians, who proved to be a war party from Red Cloud's people. A running fight ensued for several miles, the Pawnees defeating them, killing one of their number and capturing several horses.

The killing of the man seems worth recording in detail. One of the scouts that year was a half breed Pawnee whose father was a Spaniard. His name was Baptiste Behale and he was government interpreter at the Pawnee agency. When he enlisted he took with him his bow and a quiver full of arrows. When starting after the Indians that morning, he took his bow and arrows and left his gun in camp. The Sioux killed was armed with bow and arrows and after his horse had been shot he started to run on foot, shooting his arrows at the scouts until all were gone, when Baptiste, who was close to him, shot him with an arrow. It struck him under the right shoulder, went clear through his body and came out low down on the left side. He stopped, took hold of the spike end of the arrow, pulled it through himself, fitted it on to his bow, shot it back at Baptiste, and fell over dead. Baptiste threw himself flat down on his horse's neck and the arrow whizzed over his body about two inches too high. For a time, this put an end to the raiding of the graders' camps and nothing was too good for the Pawnee scouts.

When the two companies under Captains Arnold and Murie got back from Fort Sedgwick with their new guns, Captains North and Morse went there. On the second day, when they were within ten miles of Sedgwick but on the north side of the river, which was very high, some horsemen were seen across the river. Through the field glasses it was plain that they were part of a company of cavalry from Fort Sedgwick and while the Pawnees were looking at them, about a hundred hostile warriors dashed over the hills from the south and attacked the soldiers. They ran for the fort and the scouts started to cross to the river, to go to their assistance. They plunged off the bank into swimming water and were swept downstream for some distance and on to a sand bar on the same side of the river they had started from. Three of the horses were drowned and all the ammunition paper cartridges was wet. They were thus helpless. The Indians chased the soldiers to the fort killing nine of them.

The scouts kept on up the river on the north side and camped opposite the fort. The next morning they got a flat boat belonging to the government, tied some lariats to it, put their guns on board and the two officers got into the boat. The men grabbed the ropes, gave a war whoop and plunged in, to tow the boat across. In some places the water was swimming deep, but most of the way they could wade.

The carbines to be received in exchange for the muzzle loaders were old guns and many of them were defective. It was necessary to examine each one to see that all was right with it. The ordnance sergeant would hand Captain North a carbine. He would put a cartridge in the breech, throw down the lever of the breech-block and if the shell slipped through all right, he would pull up the lever and the shell would be forced into the barrel of the gun. Many of the guns did not work and the shells did not go in. When one of these was found, it was handed back and another was tried. General Emory was in command at Fort Sedgwick at this time and he came over to the store house where the carbines were being examined. When Captain North received one of the guns in which the cartridge stuck and handed it back to the sergeant, General Emory said: What is the matter with that gun? He was told the shell stuck. He said, Let me see it and took it. The shell was about half way into the chamber. He took hold of the lever and gave a quick jerk and the breechblock struck the rimfire cartridge with so much force that it exploded and the whole charge of powder blew out into his face. Fortunately he was wearing glasses and they saved his eyes, but the blood spurted from his face in streams. He had nothing further to say and left the scouts to select their own guns. It took two days to get the guns, ammunition, rations and forage and to haul it across the river in the boat.

The fight the scouts had on the way to Fort Sedgwick was the only attack on the hostile Indians that up to this time during that year had been in any way successful and the only engagement in which any of the hostiles had been killed. The Sioux were not aware that

77

the Pawnees had taken the field against them and were greatly surprised to see their old enemies in that part of the country. From that time they became more cautious and their raids on the road became less frequent.

About this time General Sherman and General Augur arrived at Julesburg on a tour of inspection, the destination of the former being Denver, while the latter was on his way to inspect all the posts of the department. Major North was detailed, with two companies at Julesburg, to accompany General Augur on this trip. The command marched up the South Platte river to a point in Colorado, about two hundred miles west of

Julesburg and thence farther up the river to the mouth of Crow creek and thence up this stream to Cheyenne pass, in Wyoming, where a fight took place with a small party of Arapahoes, who had been up in the vicinity of Fort Casper and were coming south.

An advance guard of the Pawnees attacked them, killing two warriors and taking one prisoner, who was the first warrior that had been captured alive in any of Major North's campaigns. This warrior claimed to be one of the group led by the Arapaho Friday, who was living at Fort Casper with his little band. The prisoner was later killed while trying to escape.

Shortly after this fight, some of the scouts were ordered back to the line of the Union Pacific railroad to guard a camp at Granite canyon, eighteen miles west of where Cheyenne City was afterwards built.

Two or three days after camping there, Frank North and his brother Luther, with some men and wagons set out for Fort Sanders to get rations and forage.

On the second day, when they were within three or four miles of Sanders, Frank and his brother rode on ahead, and just as they were riding up to the officers' quarters at the fort they saw eight or ten Indians riding away to the south as fast as they could go. The officer in command, who knew Frank, came out to meet them. He was laughing and said, pointing toward the disappearing Indians, There go Little Crow and some of his warriors. He is an Arapaho. He came up here to make a complaint against the Pawnee scouts for killing a couple of his warriors over at Cheyenne pass. I told him that his warriors had some mules that had been taken from emigrants over on the Laramie river. Then he said that he would like to meet the white Chief of the Pawnees; he would fix him. It was about that time that Frank and Luther had come into sight and the officer pointed to them and said, There comes Major North now, you can talk to him.

Little Crow said nothing further and seemed to have pressing business somewhere else, for he rode away from there in a hurry.

The scouts remained at Granite until the fourth of July (1867). They then moved up to the point where the city of Cheyenne now stands. General Augur, who had returned from his inspecting tour, had arrived at this point with his escort. General Grenville M. Dodge, chief engineer of the Union Pacific, together with a number of other well-known railroad officials, had also reached this place with teams from the end of the track. They decided to locate a town here, and having selected the site they had a celebration over the event.

Major North went into camp here, and furnished an escort of twenty-five of his Pawnees to protect General Dodge and the surveyors in their work of laying out the town of Cheyenne, as it was to be named. The survey occupied two weeks, at the end of which time the major with his two companies proceeded down the old Cheyenne pass emigrant route to Pine Bluffs and there left one of the companies to protect a camp of graders. The other company he stationed at Point of Rocks, twelve miles further east, to protect another camp of graders. He now went alone to the end of the track, four miles east of the present location of Sidney, and here he found the other two companies of the Pawnees with the track-layers. Before long he received orders to send one of these companies to the Laramie plains to protect the graders who were at work there.

Thus all summer long the Pawnee battalion continued to do duty along the Union Pacific road for a distance of three hundred miles from Plum creek to the Laramie plains. They had many skirmishes with the hostile Indians and frequently followed them on long rides after stolen horses and mules, which they usually recovered.

About the first of August the Cheyenne chief, Turkey Leg, made a raid on the railroad at a point about four miles west of Plum creek station, where his party ditched a west-bound freight train, killing most of the train men and scalping one of them alive. They broke open the box-cars and secured a large quantity of plunder of every description and burned part of the train.

Major North was immediately telegraphed to, at the end of the track and asked to bring down a company of his Pawnees. The nearest company available was stationed twelve miles west of the end of the track, and about two hundred and twenty miles from Plum creek. He telegraphed orders for cars to be in readiness at the end of the track, to transport the company to Plum creek. He went with them.

A few days after the scouts reached Plum creek the Cheyennes came back for more plunder and the scouts set out to meet them.

When Major North with Captain Murie and his forty Pawnees crossed the river, he found the Cheyennes on the south side of Plum creek. There were one hundred and fifty of them. Near the old stage station was an old bridge and they met near this. Frank North and a dozen of his men crossed the bridge but the rest of the Pawnees tried to ford the creek and their horses mired down in the mud. The men jumped off their horses and ran up the bank on foot. The Cheyennes were close to them and at the first volley the Pawnees killed seven of them. The Cheyennes turned and ran back toward the hills where their women were and, as soon as the Pawnees could get their horses out of the mud, they followed them. When the Cheyennes got to their women and children they stopped and fought, while the women and children threw off the packs and mounted horses and ran away. After that it was a running fight all the afternoon and at night, when the Pawnees turned back, they had three prisoners, a woman, a boy and a girl, but in crossing the Platte river in the dark the little girl, who was perhaps ten years old, got away and in some manner found her way back to her people and was living long afterwards, perhaps until 1920.

A short time after this fight, generals Sherman, Harney, Terry, Augur and Sanborn, of the army, and N. G. Taylor, Colonel Tappan, and Senator Henderson came to the North Platte to hold a council with the Brules Sioux under Spotted Tail, Man Afraid of his Horses, Man that Walks under the Ground, Pawnee Killer, Standing Elk and other chiefs of the Brules and with Turkey Leg and other chiefs of the Cheyennes. Major North went to North Platte on the train with the commissioners and in the council tent met Turkey Leg, who knew him from having seen him in the fight at Plum creek. He asked through an interpreter about the prisoners Major North had and said he had some white prisoners that he would exchange for them. Major North agreed to the exchange and Turkey Leg sent a messenger to his camp on Medicine creek and brought in three girls, two boys and a baby. A few days later North took his two prisoners to North Platte and the exchange was made at the council, which was held in the railway eating house. Two of the girls were named Martin and had been captured several months before, a few miles south of Grand Island, the other girl and two boys were thought to have been captured on the Solomon river.

Turkey Leg's reason for wanting to exchange them was that the Cheyenne boy was his nephew.

This nephew lived for many years with the northern Cheyennes and from the circumstances of his capture as a boy, he was called Pawnee. He was a quiet man, who was held in high respect by the tribe. He died a few years ago, a fairly old man.

The girl grew to be an old woman. She escaped while the Pawnees were crossing an island in the Platte river and from this fact was named Island Woman. She married White Frog, an important man among the northern Cheyennes who was the chief priest of the Massaum ceremony.

The peace council which took place between Mr. Wilson, the commissioner of Indian affairs, generals Sherman, Harney and Augur and others and the Indians is said to have been one of the largest Indian councils ever held. The treaty then made gave over all the land north of the North Platte river to Spotted Tail, Red Cloud, Turkey Leg and other chiefs-the Sioux and the Cheyennes.

About the first of October, Major North received orders to concentrate his battalion at Cheyenne, preparatory to making a trip to the Powder river country as an escort to the paymaster, but the ranchmen in the vicinity of Laramie and along the Platte river, in view of the treaty just made, protested to General Augur against sending the Pawnees into the Powder river country and declared that the appearance of the Pawnees in their territory would quite certainly lead to an outbreak among the Sioux. The Pawnees were not sent, but returned to Fort Kearny.

It was while the Pawnees were there that a number of well-known capitalists and others interested in the Union Pacific railroad, then just being built, came out to see the country. None of them knew anything about the west, but each one wished to kill a buffalo. They were taken in charge by Major North and his brother and with their Pawnees went south toward the Republican river. Among these men were Sidney Dillon, Oakes Ames, Thomas A. Durant, C. S. Bushnell, George Francis Train and others whose names are forgotten. Ambulances were taken along for them to ride in until buffalo were found, when they were to be provided with saddle horses.

Fifteen miles from Fort McPherson they found a band of about one hundred buffalo and Mr. Dillon, Mr. Durant and Mr. Train mounted their horses to join in the chase. The rest of the party stayed in the ambulance and watched the fun. Luther North had picked out a good reliable buffalo horse for Mr. Dillon, had explained to him as well as he could what he ought to do, and given him his own revolver. They came as near to the herd as they could without frightening them. Frank North gave the word and the chase was on. The ground was dry and by the time the buffalo were overtaken, the air was so filled with clouds of dust that it was hard to see a buffalo until one was within a few feet of it. Luther North's horse was a very fast one and he overtook the buffalo before anyone else and tried to cut one out and get it away from the dust to a place where the people in the ambulance might have a good view of it. Just as he succeeded in getting a fine three-year-old heifer out to the edge of the herd, his horse stepped in a hole and fell, and that ended his hunt. The horse jumped up and ran away after the herd and he was left on foot. About this time Mr. Dillon went past. He was not a very good horseman and had perhaps lost his stirrups at the first jump and when he went by Luther he was holding on to the pommel with one hand and in the other was the revolver sticking straight out to the right and the bridle reins were flapping on the pony's neck. It was doing its best to overtake the buffalo, but like Luther North's horse, it found a hole and went down and Mr. Dillon was badly bruised, but no bones were broken. The men caught the horses after a long chase.

In the meantime the herd scattered and the Indians succeeded in getting a couple of old bulls back near the ambulance where an Indian killed one with bow and arrow. He shot him with two arrows; the first one was driven in up to the feathers, and the second clear through the body and dropped out on the opposite side. Mr. Durant killed one buffalo and the scouts killed a number.

These strangers were then given every opportunity to hunt with comparative safety, under the protection of the Pawnee scouts. After they had killed all the buffaloes they desired, some of them expressed a wish to see some hostile Sioux and if possible, to witness a fight with them. As it turned out their wish was gratified.

Major North presently returned with his command to Fort Kearny, where the Pawnees remained until mustered out on the first of January, 1868. Major North, however, remained out of service only a month.

CHAPTER XII

In February, 1868, Major North received orders to reorganize two companies of the scouts, as their services were still needed for guard and patrol duty along the line of the Union Pacific. He accordingly enlisted two companies, A and B, the former commanded by Captain Morse and the latter by Captain Matthews; the two companies being called a battalion, as before. The battalion was soon put in the field. Major North's orders were to patrol one hundred miles of the railroad from Wood river station to Willow island. Every week a patrol was sent over the one hundred miles to look for the trails of Indians.

In the month of July, Major North took a detachment of the scouts twenty-five from each company and went south on a scout to the Republican river. On the way they were joined by the Pawnee tribe who were out on their annual summer buffalo hunt on their familiar hunting ground along the Republican river. With the Pawnees were some Omahas, Winnebagoes and Poncas, the whole number of Indians being about five thousand.

After a time buffalo were found and Major North concluded to return to the railroad, but before starting he determined to take twenty-five of his scouts and make a good buffalo killing, as he wished to bring back some fresh meat for those scouts who were on duty along the line of the railroad.

Major North, accompanied by Captain Morse, accordingly rode out from camp early one morning, with twenty-five of his scouts and made a successful buffalo surround on Mud creek, four miles from camp. After killing a good number of the buffalo the scouts became scattered, as often happens in making a surround.

Major North, who had ridden off to one side in pursuit of a cow he had wounded, was interrupted in the chase by one of the Pawnees who galloped up to him and said, The Sioux are after us.

The Major looked in the direction in which he pointed and seeing a party of Indians said, They must be Pawnees.

No! No! They are Sioux! replied the scout rather impatiently.

I guess you're right, said the Major as he looked again and saw the Indians still at a distance, but galloping rapidly towards them, We better get out of their way.

The Major and the scout thereupon galloped across a ravine and up the side of a hill, where they overtook two of the Pawnee scouts and told them to prepare to fight if the Sioux should overtake them. Just about this time Captain Morse and four scouts, who had also received the alarm, came running out of a ravine nearby and Major North called to them to join his party. The united force now numbered nine men Major North, Captain Morse and seven scouts.

The meeting was none too soon, for by this time the Sioux were near enough to begin firing. There were about one hundred of them, from Spotted Tail's camp near North Platte City. Major North and his little force retreated to a ravine and, sheltered there, managed to hold the enemy at bay. There was no possible chance to run away, for they were completely surrounded. Their only hope of escape was that assistance should come.

Among the charging Sioux there was one man who appeared to be the leader or chief and who carried a small American flag, perhaps captured in some fight with the United States soldiers. Frank North felt that if this man were killed, the others might lose some of their courage. He left his men and Captain Morse where they were and crept some distance up the ravine. He finally got within about two hundred yards of a little hill where the Sioux were grouped and shot this man off his horse. When this happened, the others rode back over the hill and out of sight and Frank ran back to his men. The Indians soon returned, however, and surrounded them and kept them penned up there all the afternoon.

Meantime, the main body of the Sioux, numbering five hundred warriors, had attacked the main camp of the Pawnees, who withstood their assault and drove them back a short distance. A pitched battle followed; first one side would retreat and then the other. It was a give and take fight, back and forth, which lasted for five hours. Yet little by little, the Pawnees kept driving the Sioux and finally they forced them past the ravine where Major North's party was surrounded by the other Sioux, who now were compelled to retreat with the main body of their people.

This freed Major North and his men who had had a long fight, with no little hardship. Three of the scouts were wounded, two severely, and six of their nine horses were killed. It was a very hot day and the party had all suffered greatly for lack of water- particularly the wounded men. On emerging from the ravine, none of them could speak above a whisper, so parched were their throats.

The Pawnees at the village supposed that they had all been killed and their appearance once more among them was the occasion for great rejoicing. The next morning Major North and his fifty scouts started on their return to the railroad, which they reached without further adventure.

Nothing of importance or interest occurred until about the middle of October, when the Indians made a raid near Sidney and captured some horses from the ranchmen in that vicinity.

General Augur telegraphed to Major North to ship one company of scouts to Potter station, and join Major Wells, of the Second cavalry and to scout the country north in search of the band of Indians who had stolen the horses. Upon reaching Potter station, Major Wells' detachment, with the scouts proceeded to Court House rock on the North Platte, where, on the north side of the river, they discovered the Indians driving off the stolen stock.

The river was high and full of floating ice, but Major North sent a detail of scouts under command of Lieutenant Becher across the stream and they succeeded in killing two of the Indians and recapturing the stolen horses and several Indian ponies.

Major Wells then returned to Sidney and Major North marched down the North Platte to Ash Hollow. Crossing the stream there, he went to Ogallala and a little later to Fort Kearny where the battalion was disbanded on the first of January, 1869.

Major North was retained in the service by General Augur through the winter. He was given charge of the horses, to keep them in condition and have them ready for the Pawnees when spring opened again.

CHAPTER XIII

In the year 1868, business matters made it impracticable for Luther H. North to go out with the Pawnee scouts, yet he had his share of excitement about hostile Indians and abundant work in the effort to recover from them horses taken from settlers and others.

At this time it was a practice of the various Sioux tribes, whose agencies were situated in northern Nebraska and in Dakota, frequently to go south to the Pawnee agency or the settlements to take horses, which they drove north to various Sioux agencies, where usually they were easily hidden. Sometimes the white owners of the horses, if they supposed they knew to what point the animals had been taken, would visit that agency and endeavor, with the help of the United States Indian agent, to recover their property. Occasionally the effort was successful; more often it was not. Usually the agent knew nothing of what had taken place and his enquiries did not always produce information.

After a raid on the settlements when horses were taken, it was usually not difficult to raise a party to follow the horse thieves, but often the members of such parties were very careless about arming themselves, not seeming to realize the recapture of the horses might involve a fight. The Indians were armed with rifles of one sort or another and with bows and arrows, which last, in experienced hands, were about as effective arms as the revolvers or the muzzle-loading shot-guns of that day.

In July, 1868, a war party of Sioux from Spotted Tail's camp made a raid near the Pawnee village and ran off a number of horses owned by a white settler, Allan Gerrard. He got together eleven men and followed them, sending word to the reservation and neighboring settlers as to what had taken place. A long pursuit by Gerrard's party and by another group of seven, led by Luther North, was unsuccessful in recovering the horses. North's party, however, overtook one of the two parties of Indians. This group numbered thirty-five warriors, well-armed, several with repeating rifles, while of North's party he alone carried a breech loading rifle and a Colt's revolver. The other six men had three muzzle-loading shot-guns and three muskets. With such odds against them the whites could not fight. In July he went south with his brother Frank on a buffalo hunt with some railroad men. Of some other experiences had during the same year, Luther North shall tell in his own words:

"In October, 1868, the Indians made another raid on the settlers and took some horses from them, and again a mob of us started after them. I think I am right in calling it a mob, as there was no discipline or organization, no leaders; we just went, every fellow for himself. There were about thirty in the party, and I had said that if we did not overtake the Indians before night that I was coming back.

"We followed the trail up Beaver creek until night. The next morning sixteen of the party turned back. I had intended to go back with them but Allan Gerrard asked me to go on for another day, and I agreed. We followed the trail nearly to the head of Beaver creek, where it turned to the north through the sand hills. We followed on until dark, when we camped. A bad thunderstorm came up in the night and the horses broke loose and ran away. In the morning I was the only one who had a horse. The other horses had gone only a short distance and I soon found and drove them to camp.

"We then followed on after the Indians, and before noon reached the Elkhorn river. Our horses were pretty tired and we had nothing to eat. Gerrard had brought along some flour, but no salt or baking powder, and we had eaten everything else that we had except the coffee. We mixed some dough, which we wrapped around the ends of sticks and baked by holding it over the fire. After resting for a couple of hours, someone proposed that we turn back for home. Everyone was in favor of this except Gerrard. He wanted to go on. I told him I preferred to return, but if he was going on I would go with him. Finally the crowd all decided to go back except Allan Gerrard, Samuel Smith and myself. We intended to go to Fort Randall on the Missouri river, and report our loss to the commanding officer there.

"The Whetstone agency, where Spotted Tail was located, was twenty-five miles up the river from Fort Randall, and an army officer had charge of the Indians. The second day after leaving Elkhorn river we got to the town of Niobrara at the mouth of the

Niobrara river. We were pretty hungry by this time, and we enjoyed the chicken dinner that we got there.

"The next day we went to Fort Randall. A Colonel Chambers in command there could tell us nothing and suggested that we go to the Whetstone agency and see if the officer who was acting agent there could help us find the horses. Mr. Smith was not very well, and decided to stay at Randall, while Gerrard and I went to the agency. The road was on the east side of the Missouri river, and this we were obliged to cross. There was no ferry, and we hired a man with a skiff to take us over. We put our saddles, guns and blankets in the skiff and we got in. Allan sat in the bow and I sat in the stern and led the horses, a difficult job, for the horses kept trying to climb into the boat, and came near swamping it before we got across.

"The next day we rode up the river until opposite the Whetstone agency, when we left our horses at the house of a Frenchman there and crossed over to the agency. The officer in charge sent for the interpreter, Nick Janice, who told us the horses were at the Crow Creek agency one hundred miles further up the river and that the Indians that took them did not belong to Spotted Tail's band. I was in favor of giving it up and going home, but Allan was a good sticker and wanted to go on.

"We crossed back that night to the other side of the river, and the next morning started for Crow creek, where we arrived only to find that the Indians had gone on their annual buffalo hunt. The agent said that we could not have gotten the horses anyway; that the Indians had stolen his saddle horse when they started on the hunt. He was from the East and did not know much about the Indians, and was somewhat disgusted with his job.

"The next morning we started back to Fort Randall, and that night stopped with a man that had married a Sioux woman. He told us there was a small band of the Indians from Crow Creek agency camped across the river from his house; that they had quite a bunch of horses and he had heard them talking of a wonderful running horse among them. One of my horses that they had stolen was a fast race horse, and we made up our minds to go over and take a look at their horses.

"This man had a skiff and after supper we borrowed it from him and crossed the river. It was a bright moonlight night. The camp of twenty-five or thirty lodges was in the timber. We walked through it, and although the dogs made a good deal of noise no one came out, and we went out on the prairie where their horses were grazing. There were, perhaps, a hundred of them, but none of ours. We left them and went back across the river. I have often wondered what we would have done if we had found our horses there, and have thought what fools we were to go poking around that camp in the night.

"We got back across the river about midnight and the next day came to the house of a Frenchman whose wife was a negro woman. By this time we were out of money, but we had a little bread and meat. The Frenchman had a double log house, in one end of which he lived, and in the other end he said we could sleep. We had given him what money we had for some hay for our horses, and had spread our blankets on the floor to sleep on, when he came in and said supper was ready. Allan told him we had no money, but that we would be all right as we were. The Frenchman went out and had a talk with his wife, and came back and again invited us to supper. When we got to their end of the house, Allan told the woman that we had no money. She said, 'Oh that's all right; it seems too bad to see poor white folks starving to death in a civilized country.' We had fried chicken for supper, and it tasted mighty good to us.

"The next day we got to the river opposite the Whetstone agency, and I stayed there with the horses while Allan went over to see the agent. There was a rope ferry across the Missouri at this point, and the ferryman who took Allan across the river went with him to the agency, leaving his boat until they were ready to come back. While I was waiting a team of horses hitched to a spring wagon and driven by an Indian boy, came up from Fort Randall. In the wagon were two very pretty girls sixteen and eighteen years of age. They were the daughters of a Frenchman named Beauvais, and their mother was a Sioux woman that Beauvais had married. He had taken the girls to St. Louis when they were four and six years old, and put them in a convent, where they had been for twelve years and had now come home. Neither of them could talk the Sioux language. The older girl had asked me if I knew where the ferryman was, and when I told her, she told me who they were. She seemed to be very much excited and was very glad to get home to her people. In an hour or so the ferryman and Allan put in their appearance, and Allan and I started for Fort Randall.

"About eighteen months later I was at the Whetstone agency and while in the store of the trader a Sioux woman came in. She was dressed as an Indian woman, wearing a black calico shirt, buckskin leggins and skirt, with a blanket wrapped around her. She walked past me and up the counter, where she bought some things, after which she went out. I asked the clerk if she was one of the Beauvais girls, and he said she was; But she can talk English, I said. Yes, he replied, but she won't, she is married to a big buck Indian and lives in a teepee. This was the older girl. The younger girl, I was told, had married a white man and followed the white man's ways.

"When we got to the river opposite Fort Randall we left our horses and crossed in a skiff, and after various adventures set out for the Pawnee agency, which we reached nearly four weeks after we had left it.

"Between Christmas and New Years the Indians made another raid and took two horses from me and two from the man that carried the mail between Columbus and Genoa. These horses were taken out of the agency stable. I wrote to Colonel Chambers at Fort Randall giving him a description of the horses and asking him to look out for them, as I was sure they had gone to the Whetstone agency. In about two weeks I got an answer saying that he had two of the horses, one of mine and one belonging to Mr. Regan, the mail carrier. Colonel Chambers said that he liked my horse and that if I didn't care to come after him he would send me two hundred and fifty dollars for him. The horse had been presented to me, and, of course, I did not want to part with him, and decided that I would go after him, and Mr. Regan said he would go along.

"We started on the eighteenth of January, 1869. We went to Sioux City by railroad, and from there to Fort Randall by stage. I went at once to Colonel Chambers. He said that the horses were there, but that it would be necessary for me to get an order from the acting agent at Whetstone agency before he let me have them. I told him that I had no way of getting to the agency, and he said that I could take my horse and ride up there and get the order for the two horses, and he would turn them over to me.

"Leaving Mr. Regan at the fort, I went up to the agency. The weather was very cold. I crossed the river on the ice and went up on the east side, and when I got opposite the agency I left my horse with a man who lived there and walked across the river. It was about noon, and I went to the office and found the lieutenant who was acting agent, introduced myself, and stated my business. He said he was very busy and asked me to come around later. I was hungry and started out to find some place to eat. I hadn't gone far when I met Nick Janice, who asked me to have dinner with him, which I did. After waiting at his house for about an hour, Nick and I went back to the agent. He again put me off and asked me to come back at six o'clock. As Nick and I started back for his house, I said, What is the matter with that fellow, he does not act as though he wants to give me an order for the horses? Nick laughed and said, I guess they don't want you to take that horse away. Didn't they make you an offer for him? This made me pretty angry, and I told Nick I was going back. He went with me, and when we got to the office I told the lieutenant that I was in a hurry and wanted the order for the horses. He said, I have been looking over your letter and in it you say that the bay horse has both hind feet white. Now, the horse I got from the Indians has only one white foot. He is down to Fort Randall. When he got that far I interrupted him. I said, The horse you got from the Indians has two white feet. He is not at Fort Randall, but is in my possession, and I am going to take him home and I don't care whether you give me an order for him or not. He hesitated for a minute, then turned to his clerk and told him to write me an order for the two horses. I took the order, and I am very much afraid that I forgot to thank him for it.

"That evening after supper Nick and I went over to the trading post. The store was full of Indians. In the back end of the room there was a big stove, which stood out from the wall about four feet. I walked back and sat down in a chair behind the stove. Some of the

Indians asked Nick who I was. He told them what I had come for, and instead of letting it go at that, he said, He is from the Pawnees and was with the Pawnee scouts that killed Spotted Tail's brother at Ogallala. This certainly started something. The Indians crowded up toward the stove. I didn't understand what Nick had told them, but knew that something was up. They were growing more excited every minute, and tomahawks and knives were brandished, and they were crowding up close to me. I was trying to pretend that I did not know what was wrong, and was wondering what was best to do.

"There was a window in back of the stove, and I made up my mind that if any one of them made a pass at me, I would start the old six-shooter and jump through the window. I noticed one big fellow pushing through the crowd. He had a tomahawk that he had been smoking. He was talking very excitedly, and I had about made up my mind that he was the man I would take the first shot at, when he pushed the Indians nearest to me to one side, and put out his hand to shake with me. I shook hands with him. Then he held out toward me the tomahawk he was smoking, and I smoked with him. He was talking all the time and the others quieted down and soon began to leave the store. All of this time Nick was standing there as white as a sheet. I guess he was as badly scared as I was. I asked him how this man kept them from killing me, and he replied that he told them that it would be foolish to kill me; that the troops that were there and the soldiers from Fort Randall would attack their camp and kill their women and children. After the others had gone the Indian bade me goodbye and followed them.

"I stayed with Nick overnight, and the next morning started back to Fort Randall. Nick thought that some of the young fellows might follow or waylay me, but I reached the fort all right. The next morning Mr. Regan and I started home. We went down the east side of the Missouri river, as the snow was deep and there was no road on the west side. We got to the Yankton Indian agency at noon the first day, and stopped there to get dinner and feed our horses. They had no grain there, but had some wheat. I was afraid to give my horse much of it, and warned Regan not to feed his horse too much, but he gave her a big feed. When we had ridden about two hours that afternoon she was taken sick, and before we could get to a house she died. Regan looked down at her and said, Two hundred dollars for the mare, two hundred dollars for the horse they stole, two hundred for expenses; I'll have a bill of six hundred dollars against the government. It's singular how we can figure these things out, ain't it, Mr. North? He then walked on with me until we came to a stage station. I left him there and went on alone. When I got to Sioux City there was not much snow, so I cut across country from there. I crossed the river and stayed overnight in Dakota City.

"The next morning I started across country for the Elkhorn river, where there were a few settlers and I thought I might find a place to stay overnight. I followed a wagon trail-just a few tracks. The weather was very cold, but here there was no snow on the ground as there had been farther up the Missouri. When I had ridden about ten or fifteen miles it began to snow and the wind commenced to blow. I met a man with a team going to Dakota City, and he told me it was thirty miles to the first house, and the road was hard to follow. That did not sound good to me, and I had not gone far after meeting him when the storm developed into a blizzard and I could not see the road at all.

"The horse I had at this time was perhaps the best that I ever owned, and I knew that I must trust to his instinct and intelligence to reach a house somewhere. I gave him his head and started him on a lope. He put his head down—so he could see the wagon track, I think—and never slackened his speed till we came to a house on a little creek that ran into the Elkhorn. We made the thirty miles in a little less than three hours, and how he ever managed to find the way was and is a mystery. The country was very rough and the road wound around the heads of ravines and up over big hills. Sometimes we were facing the wind and I thought he had lost the road, but soon he would make a turn and the wind was on my back. In the house that I came to livek, a German who had a shed built of straw, where he had two horses and a cow. It was a good warm place, and after I got the saddle off my horse I put in about two hours in rubbing him dry. These people lived in a dugout in the bank of a ravine. There was only one room in the house, and they had only one bed. They had a couple of small boys, and I slept with them on the floor. We had one featherbed over us and another under us and slept very comfortably.

"The blizzard kept up all night and all next day, but cleared up in the evening. I stayed another night and then started for home. I knew that it was about forty-five or fifty miles to Columbus straight across the country, but the country was rough and there was no road, and the snow was now quite deep. For this reason I followed up the Elkhorn river to the mouth of Union creek, then followed up that stream to a settlement that is now the town called Madison. From there to Columbus was thirty-five miles, and as there was a road to follow I made it that night. I had ridden somewhere between seventy-five and eighty miles that day, and much of the way was through snow from a foot to eighteen inches deep. In these days of the automobile it is hard to understand what a lot of endurance a horse must have had to make such a trip.

"It was after dark when I got to Columbus, but as I wanted to cross the river to where my brother-in-law lived, I decided to go on that night. At Joe Baker's saloon I asked about the crossing. He said that one team that was hauling wood had broken through the ice that day, and he thought it was pretty dangerous. I learned from him where they were crossing, decided to try it and rode on. When I was about half way across I came to an open channel, but it was so dark I could not see how wide it was, and had no way of knowing the depth. My horse put his head down and sniffed at the water, but when I spoke to him he jumped off the ice into the water. It came up to the middle of his sides and was full of ice. Nevertheless, he went right on, and although the channel was fifty yards across, he came out on the road on the other side. It was a pretty hard climb up on the ice, but he made it all right, and in a few minutes we had covered the three miles to my brother-in-law's house, where I turned him loose in a warm stall with two feet of straw bedding under him.

"People nowadays can hardly understand what our saddlehorses meant to us in those days. I doubt if today one could find a horse that, even in daylight, would take the plunge into icy water that he took when it was pitch dark, and he never hesitated a moment. This horse was high-strung, but gentle, was very fast, and there seemed to be no limit to his endurance. I called him Mazeppa, and the Indians called him a'di kah tus, buck antelope, because they said his face was like an antelope's."

CHAPTER XIV

In February, 1869, Luther North with one company of fifty scouts was ordered to Fort McPherson to join a winter campaign into the Republican country. Major Noyes was in command. This was A company of scouts, with North as captain and Fred Matthews as lieutenant.

They reached Fort McPherson, where they drew arms, ammunition, rations and forage and went into camp on the river. North was allowed two wagons to carry forage, rations and camp equipment, but was not allowed any tents. It rained all day, turning to snow in the evening. They spent a bad night and in the morning started for the old Jack Morrow ranch, where they were to turn south toward the Republican. Major Noyes had been gone several days and they were to follow and join him somewhere on the Republican. It was still snowing when they started, and the wind soon began to blow so hard they could not see much. They managed to get to the John Burke ranch where horses and mules were put in some sheds and the men got in some out-buildings and managed to keep from freezing.

They had expected to find plenty of buffalo in the country, but saw none and killed only a single antelope. When the scouts overtook Major Noyes he was out of rations and had killed no game and had turned back to the fort. He had with him two troops of cavalry and they had no tents. Luther North gave him almost all the rations of the Pawnees and they went into camp with the understanding that in the morning they would start for Fort McPherson.

Next morning it was snowing hard, but they started. By the time the high tableland was reached, the wind was blowing a gale, and the trail made by the cavalry was covered and could not be seen by the Pawnees. The cavalry horses were in much better condition than the Indian ponies and made much faster time. Luther North sent ahead a man on foot to follow the road. About noon it became very cold and the men began to freeze. Before starting, Major Noyes had said they would camp that night on the Frenchman's Fork, but

North knew there was no wood where the road crossed the Frenchman.

About the middle of the afternoon one of the Pawnees rode to Captain North and said, "I think we are near a canyon where there is plenty of wood." He was told to go ahead and find it and they would follow. He turned to the left of the trail and was lost to sight in a minute, but they followed in the direction he had taken and in a few minutes the man appeared and said he had found the place. They soon reached the head of a canyon where there was plenty of wood and grass, and very good shelter for the horses.

The Indian who found this canyon was the company's first-duty sergeant and was a very wonderful man. His name was Ku-ruks-u-ka-wa-di, Traveling Bear. As soon as the wagons came in, he took some men with axes and cut poles and stood them up like lodge poles; took the covers off the wagons and stretched them around the poles, making a lodge. While he, with one or two men, was doing this, he set other men to work scraping the snow off the ground and as soon as the lodge was up he had men cut rye grass with their butcher knives and spread it in the lodge for beds. Then he built a fire in the center. Then robes and blankets were spread down and in an hour they were perfectly warm and dry. The men took their blankets and some pieces of canvas and put up lodges for themselves, so all were comfortable, except for their frost bites.

The next morning was bright and clear but very cold. Luther North and his scouts went down to the Frenchman river where Major Noyes was found in camp on the open prairie. More than fifty of his horses and several of his mules had frozen to death. They had burned some of the wagons; and many of the men, including Major Noyes, were badly frostbitten. The Pawnees were all in good shape and Luther North took them down to the river which he found frozen hard enough to support a horse; but many of the horses were unshod and the shoes of those that were shod were so smooth that they could not stand up on the ice. North decided that the only way to cross was to chop away the ice and to ford the river. He sent some of the men back to Major Noyes to borrow his axes and set the Pawnees to work chopping out a lane. The Indians were a little awkward with the axes, but got along pretty well and by noon had cut a lane across the river wide enough for the wagons. North had two men ride ahead of each mule team and guide the lead mules. The wagons crossed without difficulty and Major Noyes complimented the Indians on their good work.

It took them three days to get to Fort McPherson, but the weather grew warmer and although for the last two days they had nothing to eat, they got through well enough. At the fort, Luther North drew tents, rations and forage and went into camp on an island in the Platte, wishing to build up their very thin horses for the summer campaign.

On the first of March, 1869, Major North organized three companies of the Pawnees, fifty men to each company. His officers were Luther H. North, Captain Cushing, and Captain Murie, with Lieutenants Becher, Matthews and Kislingberry.

The following May, when the Norths with one company of scouts were traveling up the North Platte river about opposite Court House Rock a curious incident happened. Just as they were going into camp one afternoon, they saw two mounted men on the north side of the river. The men were just passing out of sight behind an island that was covered with willows and it was uncertain whether they were white men or Indians. Frank North told three of the men to ride across and see who they were. The men had already unsaddled and these scouts jumped on their horses bareback. As they did so, one of them said, My horse has a sore back. Frank called out to him and said, Take my mare. This mare was a beautiful animal, cream colored, with white mane and tail. She was owned by North, was very fast and was ridden only occasionally.

The Indian took her and they went across, keeping behind the island until near the opposite shore. When they came in sight of the men, they saw that they were Sioux and started after them. The Sioux separated, one running off to the northeast, the other to the northwest. Two of the men went after one and the man riding Frank's mare after the other. They soon disappeared over the hills, but were so close behind the Sioux that it was evident they would soon overtake them. In a few minutes the two men that had followed one of the Sioux came in sight, leading the horse of the man they had been after and made signs that they had killed him. Then they rode off in the direction taken by the man riding the cream mare.

Frank North took ten men and leaving the others to finish making camp, crossed the river. Just as he reached the hills on the north side he met the three men coming back. The one that had ridden the mare was now riding a mule and had a long gash cut in one of his legs from the thigh almost to the knee and this is the story the man told.

"I was gaining on my man when he went out of sight over a sand hill. When I rode up on the hill the man was coming back up the hill on the other side with a knife in his hand. I jumped off the mare to shoot him, but the cartridge was bad and before I could throw in another cartridge he caught the gun and struck at me with his knife. I let go the gun and caught him by the wrist and threw him to the ground, where I held him till the other men came. I called to them to hurry and shoot him." Then this is what happened. A scout jumped off his horse, ran to where the two were struggling on the ground, put his gun against the Sioux's side and pulled the trigger. Probably the Indian squirmed about the time the gun went off and the shot

182 missed the man and went into the ground, but the man who had fired took one look and then ran for his horse, calling out that he shot the Sioux in the side, and that the bullet had bounced back, that the man was "medicine" tiwaruksti, and could not be killed. The one that had been holding him down jumped up, letting the Sioux go, and the Sioux promptly slashed him with the knife, picked up the gun, jumped on Frank North's mare and rode away, while the three Pawnees rode back toward camp.

Now comes an incomprehensible sequel. When Frank North met these three men and they told him their story, he sent the wounded man to camp and told the others to come back with him and show him where the fight took place. When they got there, the mule the Indian had been riding was still there. North told the men to come on and they rode toward a hill about a half mile away, where the men said the Indian had gone. When they reached the hill and looked over in the valley beyond, there stood the yellow mare and on the ground near her sat the Indian examining the Spencer carbine he had taken. When he saw Frank North and his party he took out one of his knives, drove it into the mare's heart and for the first time that day drew his bow from its case and took a handful of arrows from his quiver, and prepared to fight.

Frank North said to the Pawnees, "Now let me show you how much of a medicine man he is," and galloped straight toward him. The Indian fired one or two arrows and then turned to run. Frank North shot twice and he rolled over dead. No one seems able to explain the Indian's action. He had the fastest horse in the west and all he had to do was to get on her and ride away. The Pawnees when asked why he remained there could only say, "Maybe he was crazy."

After Major North's return from his scout up the North Platte river he was ordered to Fort Kearny and to Fort McPherson, where he reported to General Carr, who was organizing a campaign for the summer. The Fifth cavalry had recently come up from Kansas and Colorado, where it had been campaigning under Major Royall, and General Carr had been ordered to take command and prepare for an expedition to the Republican river country. Here William F. Cody was met. He had recently come up from the south.

Ten days were spent in fitting out the command for the coming campaign. The command consisted of eight companies of the Fifth cavalry and three companies of the Pawnee scouts. During their stay at Fort McPherson, General Augur and some of his officers and Lieutenant-colonel Duncan, of the Fifth cavalry, visited the post and reviewed the troops the day before they started out on the expedition.

At this review, the Pawnees made a very good appearance. They had been supplied with regular cavalry uniforms and on the occasion of this review under command of Captain Luther H. North, they were finely mounted and appeared in full uniform. They were highly commended for their soldierly appearance by the inspecting officers. This should be mentioned because fanciful and quite untrue stories have been told of this occasion, apparently with the intention of making the Indians appear ridiculous.

They went through their drill remarkably well in response to commands given in the Pawnee language, and Luther North was highly complimented by the reviewing officers for their efficiency. In the evening, after the parade, the Pawnees gave a grand dance. The next day the command started out from the post.

The route of march lay south to the Republican river, which stream they reached near the mouth of Dog creek. Thence they marched westward, following up the Republican. The Pawnees were well acquainted with this section of the country.

On this expedition the Pawnee scouts always broke camp first and always kept about three or four miles ahead of the cavalry and small scouting parties were always sent still further ahead. General Carr had with him two greyhounds and the first day after leaving the Platte river, he with his adjutant and a couple of other officers and Cody overtook the main body of the scouts. General Carr had brought his greyhounds and said that he wanted to give them a run after antelope. Asked if he thought they could catch an antelope, he said, "Yes, they can catch anything." General Carr and some of the others rode on ahead, so that if any antelope were seen they could keep out of sight until near enough to the animal to give the dogs a good start. Before long a single buck antelope was seen and by riding down into a ravine and following it for some distance, they got within about two hundred yards of him. All kept out of sight and the General's orderly dismounted and took the dogs up the bank until they could see the antelope. They started for him at once. He saw them and instead of running away, he trotted toward them. Then all the men rode up in sight. By this time the dogs were only one hundred feet from the antelope and he turned and ran the other way.

The general said, "Oh, they will catch him before he gets started." The men all gave a whoop and rode after them as fast as they could, but they were running up a hill and the horses could not make very good time and the dogs disappeared over the hill. When they were seen again they were running across a big flat and as the horses were pretty well blown, the riders stopped and watched them. The antelope soon went out of sight over a hill about a mile away, with the dogs about two or three hundred yards behind and when they reached the top of the hill they stopped for a minute and looked, then turned and came trotting back.

No one had said a word up to this time, when Cody spoke: General, he said, If anything the antelope is a little bit ahead.

Everybody laughed, except the general and at length he grinned and said, It looked that way. North never saw him take the dogs out again on that expedition. His orderly took them out quite frequently, but no one ever saw them catch an antelope, though they caught many jack rabbits.

Luther North, speaking of dogs and antelopes, writes:

"Now, here is a curious thing. I have seen some of the fastest packs of greyhounds in the west chase antelope at different times, and never saw them catch one. Colonel Clapper's crack dog along with Captain Woodson's thirteen hounds had a good start after a big buck antelope near Sidney, Nebraska, and he was so far ahead of them at the end of a mile that he stopped and looked back at the dogs; and yet there were many people at Sidney that said this pack of greyhounds caught antelope. I saw antelope run away from General George A. Custer's pack of wire-haired Scotch stag and greyhounds in the summer campaign of 1874, when we went to the Black Hills. They chased antelope many times and never caught one, though the general said they had caught many. My belief is that in the fall of the year, when the antelope were in large bands, the dogs could catch them, for then the antelope were like a flock of sheep and would get in each other's way and run against one another, but I do not believe the dog ever lived that could catch a single buck antelope that was in good condition."

One afternoon the command went into camp near the mouth of Turkey creek, and the mules were turned out to graze, a number of herders being sent out with them. Soon afterwards a small war party of Cheyennes coming from the south attempted to stampede the herd. One of the teamsters, who was doing herd duty, was killed at once and the other, shot with an arrow, came dashing into camp with the arrow still sticking in his flesh and gave the alarm. The

Pawnees instantly threw off their uniforms, and jumping on their horses without saddles or bridles, were off like the wind. Accompanied by Captains North and Cody, they reached the mule herd a long time before anybody else got there. The hostiles had not known that their old enemies, the Pawnees, were with the command and the sudden appearance greatly surprised them. They had believed that they could round up and capture the mule herd before the soldiers could reach them and this they probably would have done, except for the Pawnees. These chased the Cheyennes for fifteen miles, killing several of them.

CHAPTER XV

The troops marched up the Republican for several days, keeping scouting parties out ahead and off to the north and south every day. One night the Pawnees were camped on the south side of the river about a mile away from the cavalry and the hostile Indians made a raid on the camp, charging right through it. This charge was made about midnight and is perhaps, the only time that Indians have been known to make an attack at night. There were not more than six or seven Indians. They ran through the bunch of horses, but these were all tied and none of them got loose. There was a guard around the camp, but they dashed past the man on the east end, went right past Frank North's tent, firing into it, then past Luther North's tent, into which also they fired and out of the west end of camp. The men got after them as soon as they could, but the Indians were gone, and there was no telling which way they went. One of the scouts, Ku-ruks-tu-cha-rish (Angry Bear) was shot through the fleshy part of the thigh just above the hip joint, but was not much hurt and no one ever knew whether he was shot by the Cheyennes or by one of the Pawnees.

About twenty feet from Luther North's tent and about the same distance back from the river was a flowing spring. The water came up from the soil of the stream bottom and ran off into the river. It had cut a channel two or three feet deep. Many years afterwards, when the Pawnees and the Cheyennes had become friendly, the Cheyennes told the Pawnees that one of their men who had been in that charge was thrown from his horse and fell into this spring. He lay still in the narrow channel and said that the scouts jumped over him several times, or that several men jumped over him. He lay there until everything was quiet, when he crept down the channel to the river, then down the river until he was clear of the camp and so got away.

The next day General Carr gave orders to lie in camp that day, but that Major North should send out some scouting parties. Luther North, with Lieutenant Harvey and five men rode south, then west and then back to the river which they struck about twenty-five miles above camp. After crossing the river, Luther took his men up on the high hill, to take a look over the country before going into camp. It was just sundown.

They rode up the hill and when near the top, one of the scouts left his horse and ran up ahead on foot. The others stopped to wait for him to look over. When he had reached a point where he could see what lay beyond the hill, he sat down on the ground and motioned the others to dismount and come to where he was. They did so and when they had crept up to where they could see over the hill, it looked to them as if all the Indians in the world were there.

About a mile west of where the watchers were, the river bent around to the north and just over the hill from which they were looking was a long draw or swale that led to the river. There, strung out going down that draw was a procession of Indians the whole of Tall Bull's band of Cheyennes. Those in the lead had almost reached the point where the trail went out of sight down toward the river, and those in the rear had not passed where the scouts were and the trail they were following was not more than one hundred yards from the top of the hill. They were traveling slowly and their horses were loaded with meat and their camp equipage. They looked hot and tired.

It seemed possible that at any minute someone of them might ride up on the ridge from which the scouts were looking. None did so and finally they all passed by and out of sight to the west end of the valley. When the last of them had disappeared, it may be imagined that the white men gave each a sigh of relief.

The scouts started down the river for the camp where they had left the cavalry. When they reached there they found that another scouting party under Colonel Royall with ten of the Pawnees and Lieutenant Gus Becher in charge, had run into a small war party of Cheyennes. The soldiers and scouts chased them for several miles and killed three of them. The return of these Pawnees to General Carr's camp on the Black Tail Deer Fork caused a little temporary excitement. They charged the camp with whoops and yells and swinging their poles and lances, and the soldiers at first thought them a war party of Sioux about to make an attack. The Pawnees who had remained in camp, however, showed no surprise or excitement, nor made any preparations for battle, but themselves set up a yell. Captain Luther North explained the situation to General Carr telling him who the approaching Indians were and that their demonstrations only showed that they had had a fight and had been victorious. He had already reported his discovery of the Indians, and a large trail found near the river had also been reported.

They had to wait at the camp all day for a wagon train that was coming from McPherson, but the following day the whole command moved up the river to where the Indians had camped three days before. They took up the trail there and that day passed one of their camps and came to the second one. Along the trail was seen the print of a woman's shoe, evidence that they had a white captive.

That night Major North was ordered to take fifty of his best mounted men and three day rations and one hundred rounds of ammunition to the man and to precede the command at daylight in the morning. This was done, and after traveling about fifteen miles they came to another camp that the Indians had left the day before. On leaving this camp, the Cheyennes had separated into three parties and General Carr divided his command. With part of the cavalry and five or six Pawnee scouts under Sergeant Wallace, he took the left hand trail toward the northwest. Colonel Royall with the rest of the cavalry and Cody as guide took the right-hand trail toward the northeast, and the Norths with Captain Cushing and thirty-five scouts took the middle trail, leading straight north. This was Sunday, July 11th.

The weather was hot and they could not travel fast, but most of the time went on a slow trot. When the Norths with their Pawnees had gone perhaps fifteen miles, they were overtaken by one of the scouts that had been with General Carr, with orders to join him at once, as they had found the Cheyenne village. This man said that General Carr was concealed behind a ridge of sandhills and that the hostiles had not discovered the troops. The Norths at once turned west to join General Carr. They rode at a gallop and came up with General Carr, whose men were all dismounted and waiting. The Pawnees also dismounted and began stripping the saddles from their horses,

108

as they always rode into battle bareback, if they had time to unsaddle their horses.

When they reached the command their horses were pretty well blown and General Carr decided to wait for a time before making the charge on the village, expecting Colonel Royall to join him.

Meantime Major North looked over the ground as carefully as was possible at this distance, to decide from what direction the village might best be attacked.

After perhaps half an hour the general said that he would wait no longer, for fear the Indians might discover the troops and escape. The men were ordered to mount and they started. The village was about three miles away and as soon as they passed over the ridge of sandhills the horse herds of the camp could be seen, but not the lodges. A long valley ran down almost to the village and when the orders came to charge all broke into a run. As the Pawnees were riding bareback they outran the soldiers and reached the village a little ahead of them.

Major North, who was riding a very fast horse, was two hundred yards ahead of everyone and his brother was just ahead of the Pawnees. As Major North rode over the hill he was almost in the village. The Indians were rushing out of their lodges and five or six that had caught horses came up the hill from the village and met him. He stopped his horse and jumping off opened fire on them, but they turned and ran and he did not hit them.

An incident of this charge which seems worth relating is told by Luther North in these words:

"About half a mile from the village, and off to one side from our line, a Cheyenne boy was herding horses. He was about fifteen years old and we were very close to him before he saw us. He jumped on his horse, gathered up his herd and drove them into the village ahead of our men who were shooting at him. He was mounted on a very good horse and could easily have got away if he had left his herd, but he took them all in ahead of him. Then, at the edge of the village, he turned and joined a band of warriors that were trying to hold us back, while the women and children were getting away.

There he died like a warrior. No braver man ever lived than that fifteen year old boy."

The Indians were lying in camp that day and their horses were grazing over the prairie at some little distance from the village. It was warm and pleasant and a great many of them were lounging about in the shade of the lodges. They were completely surprised and before they could realize the situation, the Pawnee scouts and the cavalrymen had ridden into the village and the Indians became wholly demoralized. They fled, leaving everything behind them. The soldiers and the Pawnees, as they entered the village, fired volley after volley to the front, to the right and to the left, causing the greatest consternation. The Cheyennes made no resistance to the attack. Many of them fled on foot-some few escaped on their ponies, while a large number, unable to get away on horseback, dodged into ravines and little pockets and washouts in the nearest hills. All this occupied but a few moments and as the Indians had been scattered, the soldiers, in squads, began hunting them through the nearest ravines.

As the North brothers, Captain Cushing and Sam Wallace rode up to a big lodge near the end of the village, they saw on the ground a small keg of water. They were hot and thirsty; Captain Cushing got off his horse and after drinking, handed the keg to Frank North who was still on his horse. Just then a white woman came crawling out of the lodge and running to Captain Cushing fell on her knees and threw her hands about his legs. She was bleeding from a bullet wound in her breast. She was a Swede and could not speak English, and had been captured months before when these Cheyennes had raided a Swedish settlement in Kansas. Tall Bull had taken her for his wife and when the soldiers charged the camp he tried to kill her, but only made a flesh wound through her breast. The men finally made her understand that she was safe and that she should stay where she was.

After Frank North had drunk from the keg he handed it to Luther. He raised it to his lips and as he did so, an Indian who was lying in the grass about fifty yards away shot at him. Luther felt the bullet strike him in the stomach and come out of his back and almost fell off his horse. He opened his shirt and looked for blood but saw none, then when he felt his back that seemed all right. He felt a little ashamed now and looked around at the other men, but they were talking to the woman and had not seen his start. He took a drink of water and said nothing, thinking that he must have imagined it all. Before they started to leave the village Luther saw a saddled horse up the creek and rode up toward it, intending, if he could catch it, to turn loose his own mare which was pretty tired. He had gone only a short way when he saw before him a dead white woman. She had been killed with a tomahawk. It was learned that she had been taken at the same time as the other woman and when the camp was charged, the Cheyennes killed her. After catching the horse, Luther rode after his brother Frank and overtook him about half way across the camp.

Major North and his brother, Captain Luther North, with a party of Pawnees were surrounding one of the ravines into which a number of Indians had fled for safety. Among these was the noted chief, Tall Bull and his wife and child. They were mounted on a beautiful orange-colored horse, with silver mane and tail. Upon reaching the ravine he placed his squaw and child well within it out of danger, and then returned to the mouth of the ravine and killed his horse.

Frank and Luther were riding along a little ahead and to the left of their men when an Indian hidden in the ravine raised his head and fired at Frank, who threw his hand up to his face and stopped for a moment, so that Luther thought he was hit. He jumped off his horse and handing Luther his bridle rein, said: "Ride away and he will put up his head again."

Luther started the horses off on a lope and the Indian raised his head to look, but did not get it very high for Frank was ready for him and shot him in the forehead. Luther turned back and dismounted and just then an Indian woman and a little girl climbed out of the ravine where the Indian had fallen and came over to them.

She walked up to Frank and passed her hands over him and asked for pity and then talked to him by signs. He replied in the same language and pointed over to where the white woman was, telling her to go over there and wait, which she did. This woman was Tall Bull's wife and the Indian killed there was Tall Bull himself, though this was not known until three days later when they reached Sedgwick. There the interpreter, Leo Palliday, asked the woman if Tall Bull had been killed. She said, "Yes," and pointing to Frank North said, "This man killed him where I came out of the canyon."

After sending the woman away to the village, Frank and Luther went up toward the head of the canyon where their men were waiting. The canyon was about twenty feet deep here and very narrow, with perpendicular sides, and many Cheyenne warriors had run up there. They were armed with bows and arrows and whenever anyone came within sight near the canyon, they let fly their arrows. Then the scouts would run up to the canyon, push their guns over the edge, shoot and run back. After keeping this up for a time, at last, when no more arrows came up, they looked down into the canyon and saw there thirteen dead warriors and between there and the mouth of the canyon were six or seven more and in the village were about twenty dead. All these, except two, were warriors.

During the fight, one of the Pawnees of Luther North's company, Ku-ruks-u-ka-wa-di, Traveling Bear, had left his horse, which was tired out and pursued four Cheyennes, who also were on foot. They ran into the canyon just spoken of and he followed and overtook and killed all four of them and came back out of the mouth of the canyon with four scalps and four revolvers. Frank North reported this to General Carr and in his report of the battle General Carr mentioned the man for his bravery, but in some way the name was confused with the name of the man Ku-ruks-ti-cha-dish, Mad (Angry) Bear, who had been wounded in the night attack on the Republican about a week before. Later congress had a bronze medal struck for him. The name on the medal was Mad Bear, but it was given by Frank North to Traveling Bear. Mad Bear was in an ambulance the day of the battle, as he was not yet well enough to ride on horseback.

After the pursuit of the fleeing Indians, of whom a number were killed, the command finally turned back toward the village and began to gather up the horses and mules that the Indians had abandoned. There were about five hundred horses and one hundred and twenty mules. The mules they had taken from freighters and they were extra good ones. The charge into the camp was made at two o'clock and the troops returned about six. Just as they reached the village, a terrific storm of rain and hail came up and while all hands were trying to get under shelter in the lodges, Cody rode into camp. He had been with Colonel Royall and had missed the fight. Later, by Ned Buntline (E. C. Judson), he was given the credit for having killed Tall Bull, but he was not in the fight at all.

While they were waiting for the storm to pass over, Luther North told the men with him that he had supposed he had been shot when they first rode into the village and that even now he was sore and stiff. Captain Cushing picked up Luther's belt, which had a large square buckle on it, and said, "Well, you were hit; the buckle is bent where the bullet struck it." Luther then opened his shirt and found a black and blue spot three or four inches in diameter on his stomach. He also had a cut over his eye where an arrow had hit him during the fighting at the head of the canyon. No others of the Pawnee command were hurt.

The village was very rich in fancy buckskin shirts and dresses with beadwork and colored porcupine quills worked into them. There were several Navajo blankets and many fine buffalo robes, besides some money and jewelry that the Indians had taken from the colony they had massacred on the Solomon river when they took the white women. In the village the Pawnees found six hundred and forty dollars in gold, every dollar of which they turned over to the white woman that they found. This woman, whose name was Weichel, recovered from her wound and afterward married a soldier at Fort Sedgwick. The white woman who was killed by the Indians, whose name was said to be Suzannah Alderdice, was buried near where she died and the battlefield was at first called Suzannah Springs, but later was named Summit Springs by General Carr.

The day following the fight was given up to the work of destroying the village. The lodges and everything combustible were burned and in the afternoon the command moved camp about ten or fifteen miles down to the Platte river.

Tall Bull and his followers had long been a terror to the border settlements and the destruction of his village and the killing of its leader was a great satisfaction to the settlers and to the military authorities. General Carr and Major North and the entire command were highly complimented in general orders of the war department and by resolutions of thanks passed by the legislatures of Colorado and Nebraska. These follow:

Headquarters Dept, of the Platte Omaha, Nebraska, August 3d, 1869.

General Order No. 48.

The general commanding the department takes pleasure in announcing to his command the success of the operations conducted by Brevet Major-general E. A. Carr, major of the Fifth cavalry, against the hostile Indians in the "Republican country."

General Carr's command consisted of Companies "A", "C", "D", "E", "G", "H", and "M", Fifth cavalry under Majors Royall and Crittenden and one hundred and fifty Pawnee scouts under Major North.

General Carr commends the cheerful readiness and good conduct generally of all the officers and men of the Fifth cavalry, and also of the Pawnee scouts under Major Frank North. He mentions especially the bravery and gallant conduct of Corporal John Kyle, company "M", Fifth cavalry, and of Sergeant Co-rux-te-chod-ish (Mad Bear) 10 of the Pawnee scouts.

The general commanding tenders his thanks to General Carr and his command, for their patient endurance of the privations and hardships inseparable from an Indian campaign, and for the vigor and persistency of their operations, so deserving the success achieved. The following embraces but a portion of the property captured:

Two hundred and seventy-four horses; one hundred and forty-four mules; nine thousand three hundred pounds of dried meat; eighty-four lodges complete; fifty-six rifles; twenty-two revolvers; forty bows and arrows; fifty pounds of powder, etc. etc.

About fifteen hundred dollars in money was found in the camp by the soldiers, and the general commanding commends, in the warmest terms the generous-hearted feeling which prompted them to give most of it—over nine hundred dollars—to the liberated white captive, Mrs. Weichel.

By Command of Brevet Major-general Augur, George D. Ruggles, assistant Adjutant-general.

The resolutions of thanks passed, the next winter, by the legislatures of Nebraska and Colorado were sent to General Carr and Major North. The following is a copy of the resolutions passed by the Nebraska legislature:

Joint Resolution.

Returning thanks to Major General Eugene A. Carr and his Fifth Cavalry Regiment; and to Major North and his Pawnee Scouts.

Resolved, by the Legislature of the State of Nebraska, that the thanks of the people of Nebraska be, and are hereby tendered, to Brevet Major-general Carr and. the officers and soldiers under his command, of the Fifth United States cavalry, for their courage and their perseverance in their campaign against the hostile Indians on

10 Error as elsewhere noted. The Pawnee commended was Traveling Bear. the frontier of this State, in July, 1869; driving the enemy from our borders and achieving a victory at Summit Springs, Colorado territory, by which the people of the State were freed from the merciless savages.

Second. Resolved, that the thanks of this body and of the people of the State of Nebraska are hereby also tendered to Major Frank North and the officers and soldiers under his command, of the "Pawnee Scouts," for the heroic manner in which they have assisted in driving hostile Indians from our frontier settlements.

Third. Resolved, that the Secretary of State is hereby instructed to transmit a copy of the foregoing resolutions to Major General Eugene A. Carr and Major Frank North.

Wm. McLennan, Speaker of the House of Representatives.

E. B. Taylor, President of the Senate.

Approved February 23d, 1870. Attest: Thomas P. Kennard, Secretary of State.

CHAPTER XVI

About this time General Carr was relieved of the command and ordered to Fort McPherson. The troops, however, remained for two weeks at Fort Sedgwick to give the men and their horses a rest. They were then ordered out to scout for Indians who had been reported south of the Platte.

They left Fort Sedgwick under Colonel Royall and marched towards the Frenchman's Fork of the Republican river. They soon struck the trail of the Indians, who discovered the troops first and moved south, then east, and then north, making a horse-shoe trail, and giving the troops a chase of one hundred and fifty miles. They crossed the Platte river near Ogallala. The command followed the trail of the Indians still northward through the sand-hills for over two hundred miles, to the Niobrara river and beyond, but did not overtake them.

The day the command reached the Platte was very hot and dry and an example of Indian trailing was seen which Captain North may himself describe. He said, We were traveling as fast as we could, and I kept one or two of my men out ahead as trailers. We were crossing a high tableland covered with buffalo grass, when Cody rode up to me and pointing to the man ahead, asked, Does that Indian think he is following a trail? I said, Yes. He said to me, Can you see any trail? and I told him I could not. Then he proposed that we ride on and ask the man, which we did. He replied, Yes, I am following the trail. I said, The Long Hair says he doubts if there is a trail. The Indian pointed ahead, where about three miles away there was a ridge of sand hills, with a gap in the crest, and said, Tell the Long Hair that when we get there he will see. We rode on until we came to the sand hills and there were the tracks, plenty of them. Cody said, Well, I take off my hat to him, he is the best I ever saw.

Captain North gives another brief note on Indian character which seems worth quoting. He says:

"That night we got to the Platte river, after a ride of seventy miles. We were all very tired and hot and thirsty, and as the wagon train did not get in, we went to sleep hungry. One of my men, who had been my orderly, took my horse and led him away to find good grass for him, and I lay down with my saddle blanket over my head to keep the mosquitoes from eating me up, and went to sleep. About midnight my boy came and woke me, and said he had some coffee for me. I roused Captain Cushing and we followed him to the river bank, where he had a half gallon tin pail of coffee, and three hard tack for each of us. We ate them and drank the coffee, before I thought to ask the boy where his share was. He said, 'I will wait until the wagons get here.' I tell this to show how loyal these men were and how devoted to anyone they liked. He had ridden that day as far as I, and had taken care of my horse; then had hunted up fuel enough to make the coffee, and that was no small job, then had given us all he had, when he knew the wagons would not be in until the following day."

The troops returned to Fort McPherson, and were given a rest of two weeks. General Duncan now took command and marched south to Beaver creek, the force consisting of about one thousand men. This was the first scout of the Pawnees under General Duncan, and in putting out his guards he stationed them in a manner different from that followed by General Carr and Colonel Royall, and insisted that the different posts should call out the hour of the night: "Post number one, nine o'clock; all's well!" "Post number two, nine o'clock; all's well 1" etc.

Only a few of the Pawnees could speak English well enough to repeat this, and their attempts to call out the hour of the night were very amusing. It proved so absurd that the general soon countermanded his order.

On the second day out from Fort McPherson, Cody (Buffalo Bill) who was with the command as scout and guide, invited Major North to go on a hunt and accordingly they rode far ahead of the column and found buffalo abundant. About one o'clock in the afternoon, as they were on the divide not far from Beaver creek, they left their westerly course and turned south, to look for a good camping place for the command. They soon came to a deep, dry ravine, with very steep banks and for some distance hunted for a place through which they thought the wagon train could safely be brought.

"I'll stay here and direct the command to this point, said Cody, and you can ride over the hill and see if there is room for a camp."

Major North rode over the hill and was soon out of sight of Cody. He found a beautiful plateau and ample room for the large command. He dismounted and stood there holding his horse by the bit. It would have been natural to tie the animal with a lariat to let him feed and himself to have lain down, but suspecting that Indians might be near he was not inclined to take chances.

He had been there only a few minutes when, without warning, six Indians came galloping out of a little ravine just above him and not more than fifty yards distant. He was much startled at their sudden appearance and the Indians were equally surprised at seeing the major. Instead of wheeling toward him, they lay down on the opposite side of their horses and whirled them away from him and started off on a full run. Before they recovered from their surprise and turned back again, North had mounted his steed and was riding swiftly back over the hill. He called to Buffalo Bill, who jumped on his horse and joined him and then both ran their horses up the opposite side, just as the Indians—whose number had suddenly increased to thirty or forty—reached the other bank and fired several shots at them.

The two white men whirled their horses and fired back at the Indians. Meantime, the engineer corps, under Captain George F. Price, had discovered the Indians in pursuit of the two men and now hurried toward them. When the Indians saw these reinforcements they turned and ran. In all previous marches in which Major North's Pawnee scouts had served, they had al- ways been placed in advance of the column, where scouts might naturally be expected to work. General Duncan, through some original idea of his own, had just ordered them to march in the rear. Major North, unaware of General Duncan's new order, rode back to the command, expecting to find the Pawnees at the head of the column and not seeing them in their usual place, he asked General Duncan where they were and at the same time asked permission for the scouts to pursue the Indians. The general told him where they were and granted his request.

The column of six hundred cavalrymen, marching by twos, was very long and it was nearly a mile back to the Pawnees. Major North galloped his horse to the rear and when he came within sight of them, he signaled to the Pawnees by running his horse in a circle, thus indicating that he had discovered a party of enemies. The next moment the Pawnees came flying on their horses up to the major, throwing off their saddles and stripping themselves as they rode, according to their usual custom. The major informed them of the whereabouts of the Sioux and was pointing toward the place where he had discovered them, when the scouts, in looking across Beaver creek, saw a party of about forty Indians going up the opposite side of the stream. The scouts, with Major North, at their head, set out in pursuit and chased them ten or twelve miles, killing one and capturing several ponies.

The command went into camp at this point and upon resuming the march the next morning discovered an abandoned Sioux camp about three miles up the creek.

The camp had consisted of between seventy-five and eighty lodges-about five hundred people. It seemed evident that on the previous day the forty Sioux had shown themselves for the purpose of leading the Pawnees away from this village, in order to give the main body of the Sioux an opportunity to make their escape. In the village was found much abandoned material; large quantities of buffalo meat, many buffalo robes and much camp equipment and some heavy articles captured from the whites, which would have encumbered the Indians in their flight.

General Duncan detailed one company of cavalry and one company of Pawnee scouts, to follow up the trail as far as the Republican river, with instructions to return if they did not overtake the Indians before reaching the river. The two companies marched all day and part of the night, making fifty miles but without catching the Indians and the next day they returned to the command.

It was afterward learned that the Indians went north, crossing the Union Pacific railroad at Ogallala. They had traveled a distance of one hundred and sixty miles in less than two days and nights.

The command marched to the head of the Beaver creek, and crossing over to the Republican river on the north, went thence to the forks of the Republican. Here detachments were sent out on scouting duty along both forks with the purpose of driving the Indians from that part of the country and forcing them north of the railroad.

The command finally marched down the Republican again and crossed back to the Beaver, very nearly on their old trail. They discovered no Indians, except an old Sioux woman who had been abandoned by her people in their hurried flight and had become lost. When picked up by the Pawnees she was almost dead from starvation, having been in the country alone for two weeks ever since the Sioux had fled to the north with nothing to eat except a few roots which she had gathered. The Pawnees brought her into camp where she was taken care of. She was recognized by John Nelson, a scout of the command, as a distant relative of his wife, a Sioux woman. It was learned from the captive that the Indians who had abandoned her were Pawnee Killer's band and that on Beaver creek they had recently killed Buck's surveying party, consisting of eight or nine men. A number of surveying instruments had been found in the abandoned camp of the Indians.

The command now returned to Fort McPherson, where the Pawnees were mustered out. The old Sioux woman was sent to the Sioux agency at Whetstone on the Missouri river.

In the spring of 1870, acting under instructions from General Augur, Major North recruited two companies of Pawnee scouts for patrol and guard duty along the line of the Union Pacific railroad. He stationed one company at Plum creek and the other at O'Fallon's. They remained in the service until the next January, when they were mustered out. Major North, in obedience to orders, proceeded to the camp of Captain Munson, who had two companies of troops stationed on the north fork of the Loup, to act as guide and interpreter and remained there with only one interruption until the next fall.

That summer (1870) Professor O. C. Marsh, of the Peabody museum of Yale college, brought out to Fort McPherson a group of students to make a geological study of the late Tertiary beds of the Loup Fork river. Major North with two of his Pawnee scouts guided the party and its escort from the Fifth United States cavalry, through the sand hills of western Nebraska, which were then little known. The assignment to this duty was no doubt made at the suggestion of General P. H. Sheridan, in command of the Military Division of the Missouri, who was a friend of Professor Marsh. The party traveled north from Fort McPherson, crossed the south and middle Loups and returned by way of the Dismal river and the Birdwood river to the forks of the Platte and Fort McPherson.

During the winter of 1871-1872, Major North was assigned to duty at Fort D. A. Russel, in Wyoming. Two weeks after his arrival at that post the Third cavalry came up from Arizona and took station there. Red Cloud and his people, whose agency was located on the North Platte, thirty-five miles below Fort Laramie, had shown signs of hostility, and three companies of the Third cavalry, under Captain Guy V. Henry, were ordered to the agency. They made a forced march of one hundred and thirty-five miles in two days and a half. Their presence soon quieted the Indians and after remaining at the agency three weeks the detachment returned to the post.

In 1869, the Indian department was turned over to the Quakers, and all the agents appointed at the different agencies were Quakers. They were ordered to put a stop to all tribal wars.

In the fall of that year a war party of Pawnees made a raid on the southern Cheyennes in the Indian territory and took from them about one hundred and fifty head of horses. The leader of the party was (Uh-sah-wu-u-led-i-u) Big Spotted Horse, and when he brought the horses to the reservation, the agent, Major Troth, took them from him and turned them over to the chiefs, to be taken care of until such time as arrangements could be made to send them back to the Cheyennes. He called a council and told all the chiefs that they were not to go to war anymore; that all the different tribes were to be friendly with each other, and that the horses they had taken must be sent back and that the Pawnees must take them back. The Pawnees declined to do this, explaining to him that the Cheyennes would surely kill them, if they went to the Cheyenne village.

In the meantime winter set in and nothing more was done about it, until the next spring, 1870. Every now and then through the winter the chiefs who had charge of the horses reported to the agent that one of them had died, so that by the time arrangements had been made to return them, only thirty-five were left. Soon after Luther North returned from his trip to the Whetstone agency, the agent engaged him to take the horses south as far as Fort Harker in Kansas, where he should turn them over to the quartermaster, who was to send them on to the Cheyenne agency. Eight young Pawnees and one chief, Fighting Bear, went with North as helpers. All had been soldiers in his company the year preceding. This is the story of the ride as Luther North tells it:

"We started from Columbus and a number of people rode out with us to the Platte river to see us cross. The Platte was bank full, but I was now riding my own horse, and a better swimmer than he never lived, so I took the lead. We crossed about two hundred yards above where the present wagon bridge is situated, went on and crossed the south channel, and stayed that night on Clear creek.

"The next day, near the present site of Osceola, we met a herd of Texas cattle out in the hills. The cattle were strung out on the trail, and the two cowboys that were on the point did not see us until we were pretty close to them. They wheeled their horses and ran for the rear end of the herd as hard as they could go. I left the boys to bring on the horses, and I rode ahead. There were ten of the cowboys and as soon as I came to them the foreman wanted to know how many cattle I wanted. I laughed and told him I wasn't holding up cowboys, and after I had told him my business and where I was going, I gave him a few pointers about crossing the Platte river, and also directed him where to strike the trail for the Whetstone agency, the point he was headed for.

"He insisted on giving us a yearling steer to kill, and as we had no fresh meat it was very welcome. They cut the yearling out of the herd for us, and I had one of the boys, named Sa kur e a le shar, Sun Chief, run after it and kill it with bow and arrow, to show them how the

Pawnees killed buffalo. This boy, Sun Chief, was a nephew of Pita le shar, and later was head chief of the Pawnee tribe.

"About noon the second day after meeting the cowboys, we reached a little town in Kansas called Belleville and camped on a small stream just at the edge of the town. I rode over to the nearest house and explained to the woman who came to the door that the Indians were friendly, and that we would camp on the creek until toward evening, when it got cooler, and would then move on. After we had eaten, I went to sleep under a tree, and in about an hour one of the boys woke me up and said we were surrounded by white men, and that they all had guns. I got up and looked, and about two hundred yards away I saw several heads sticking up over the hill. I waved at them, and leaned my gun against the tree, and walked up to where they were. There were fourteen of them, and I told them what my business was, and asked them to come to camp and I would show them my letter of instructions from General Augur, who was in command of the Department of the Platte.

"They rode down to camp, and at the same time another party from the other side of the creek came in to the camp; there were thirty of them in all. I got my letter and handed it to a big, fat, pompous looking man, who seemed to be the leader of the crowd. He put on his spectacles and looked it over very carefully, and then said, How am I to know that you didn't write this letter yourself? We don't want any Indians around here; you get out as quick as you can. I think we ought to hang all of you, and you are no better than the Indians; or you would not be with them. By the time he finished I was pretty cross. I grabbed my gun and said: You get out of my camp, and get out quick. He opened his mouth to answer, but I jumped toward him, and poked the muzzle of my gun into his stomach and said, Go on now, and he went. I turned to the others and told them that I was on business for the government, and that I would move on when I got ready. One of the crowd said that was all right; that the fat man had no right to talk to me as he did. They all shook hands with the Indians, and there was no more trouble. Several of them had heard of the Pawnee scouts and of my brother. When we got ready to move on, about fifteen of them rode with us for eight or ten miles.

"That night we camped on the Republican river, and the next day we got to the Saline river, near where the year before, the Cheyennes had captured the two white women that we recaptured from them at Summit Springs, Colorado. While we were in camp on the Saline, two young men came into our camp, and in talking to them I found that one of them was a brother of Mrs. Alderdice that had been killed by the Cheyennes when we attacked their villages. I told him that I was the first man to get to his sister, but that she was dead when I got to her. He seemed relieved when I told him that they had not tortured or mutilated her. I told him of having seen her buried, and that one of the officers of the Fifth cavalry had read the burial service at the grave, and this pleased him.

"One day when we got to the Solomon river and had gone into camp, one of the boys went up the river and when he came back to camp there were two soldiers with him. The soldiers told me they were camped up the river about a half mile, on the opposite side of the river. A little way below their camp there was a lot of driftwood that reached across the river. One of the soldiers was hunting in the woods along the river, and came out on the bank just opposite this driftwood, and when he saw the Pawnee boy was coming across it, he pointed his gun at him and ordered him to halt but the boy kept coming right on and said, CA11 right, me Pawnee scout.' The soldier knew of the scouts, but he also knew that the scouts should be dressed in uniform, so he took the boy prisoner, and brought him to their camp. He could speak only a few words of English, but made the sergeant who was in command of the squad understand that there was a white man with them; so two of the soldiers came down to see. They said they thought the boy was lying to them, because if he was a scout he would know what the command to halt meant. I asked the boy why he didn't stop when the soldier told him to halt, and he replied, I thought if I stopped he would think I was going to run and would shoot me, but if I kept on going toward him he would know I was friendly.'

"We met no one else between there and Fort Harker, and on the seventh day I got there and turned over the horses, and got the quarter-master's receipt for them, and the next morning started back. The boys were now all on foot, but Fighting Bear and I had brought our own horses to ride back. It had taken us seven days to go down, but the boys were in a hurry to reach home, as the tribe was about ready to start on the summer buffalo hunt, and we made the return trip in five days. The distance was two hundred and fifty miles.

"I think it was the second night after we left Fort Harker that we camped on a small creek. We were close to the bank, and just as it was getting dark one of the boys saw some men down the creek. I sent a boy to find out who they were, and how many. He came back soon and said he saw ten and that they were watching our camp. We built up our campfires, and took our blankets and lay down a little way from the fire, and as soon as it began to die down a little, we crawled away into the darkness. The boy that took care of my horse saddled him. I mounted, and we moved away about a half a mile and again stopped. In about an hour we could see men around the campfire we had left. I suppose they crept up under the bank of the creek expecting to get a shot at us before we woke up, and we weren't there. About two o'clock my boy woke me and we started on our day's journey. We often started at two or three in the morning, and by six or seven we would have made twenty-five miles, when we would have breakfast, then sleep or loaf till about three in the afternoon, and then make another twenty-five miles and camp for the night.

"When the sun came up on the morning I have just spoken of, we were perhaps fifteen miles on our way, and in looking over the boys I missed Sun Chief. I asked where he was, and my boy said he guessed he was back where we had slept, that he didn't get up when we did, but that he would catch up with us when we stopped for breakfast. We were now in sight of the Republican river, and we followed it up until it was time to stop for breakfast. After we had

126

eaten I got out my fieldglass and began to look down the river for Sun Chief, and at last, when I was really beginning to get uneasy about him I saw him coming on a pretty fast run. When he reached us and had something to eat, he told his story. He said he never woke up until sunrise, and then started after us.

"There was a high divide to cross between the creek where we had camped and the Republican river, and he kept up a ravine until he came to its head and then thought he could cross the divide and get into a ravine on the other side, and thus keep out of sight, but when he was about half way across, two men rode out of a ravine facing him. He saw that they had seen him, so he kept on toward them. They were armed with Winchester repeating rifles. When they got to him one of them asked him for his bow. He handed it to him; then he wanted his arrows and Sun Chief took off his quiver and gave it to him. One of the men was talking very excitedly, and he could understand that he was in favor of killing him, but the man that had taken his bow and arrows would not consent, and finally told him to go on. He started, but when he had gone a little way the man called to him, and when he stopped the man rode up and gave him his bow and quiver full of arrows. Sun Chief took two of the arrows and gave them to the man as a present, which seemed to please him. They shook hands and said goodbye. Sun Chief said he never stopped running until he got to our camp.

"The last night we camped on a little stream below Fairmont, Nebraska, and just before we got to camp my boy, the one who took care of my horse, put his hand on his knee and limped for two or three steps. Sun Chief said, What is the matter, are you getting tired? The boy said, No, but my knee hurts. Sun Chief laughed and said, I guess you are tired out. My boy, whose name was Pe-isk-i-le-shar, Boy Chief, finally said, If you think I am tired, I will race you tomorrow from here home-about eighty-five miles. Sun Chief promptly accepted the challenge, and they agreed that they would leave the rest of the party as soon as it got light in the morning and see which would get to the agency first. I told them I would go with them as far as the Platte river, where I should leave them and go to Columbus. The others were to come on with Fighting Bear.

"We started about three in the morning, and before daylight were trotting along the side of a hill. My boy, who was jogging along by my horse touched me and said, 'There is a man ahead of us.' I stooped down and against the skyline and nearly at the top of the hill, I could see a man. He was holding a pair of mules, and his wagon was near him. The mules had probably smelled the Indians and awakened him. They were looking toward us with their ears thrust forward. I turned a little to the left and we went trotting past him about twenty feet away. I suppose he was a homesteader, just taking a claim. I never saw or heard of him again, but I guess he thought he had a narrow escape that time. At about sunrise, Sun Chief and Boy Chief increased the pace, and the others slowly dropped behind, for the country was rough up hill and down and the day was hot. At ten o'clock we reached the Blue, more than forty miles from the starting point, and here Sun Chief made a mistake. He drank cupful after cupful of water. My boy sipped a little and poured several cupfuls over his head. In a few minutes Sun Chief got very sick and threw up the water that he had drunk, and after lying in the shade for a half hour, he said, he was ready to go on. I wanted to give my horse a little more rest, so we waited a while longer, and then started on.

"We crossed the Platte river at Garner at two o'clock, and the distance from there to the agency was about fifteen miles, and almost all the way through the sand hills. I left the boys and rode down the river about eight miles to my sister's and the boys struck through the sandhills for home. I saw Sun Chief about a month afterward, and asked him how the race came out. He laughed and said, 'He beat me. I had to stop and rest.' Boy Chief got home at five o'clock, and we had stopped on the Blue nearly two hours, so the actual running time was twelve hours, and distance 85 miles."

CHAPTER XVII

In 1872, not very long after Frank North was transferred to Fort Russell, Wyoming, Luther was employed at a military camp on the north Loup. Major Switzer was in command and in June he made a scout up the south fork of the Loup, about sixty miles above St. Paul, where the trail of about twenty lodges of Indians was found. The troops camped that night on the south Loup and the next morning started to follow the trail. It led north through the sand hills and was followed to the north Loup.

Luther North was riding about three miles ahead of the command, with three of the soldiers when they rode up in sight of the Indian camp. The Indians saw them at once and while the women began to take down the lodges preparatory to moving away, the warriors jumped on their horses and charged toward the whites. The soldiers started back on a run to meet the command, while Luther North looked over the camp through his field-glass, to learn how many Indians there were. The camp was about a mile away and as Luther was riding his fleet horse, Mazeppa, he knew that he could run away from them at any time. Of the soldiers with him, one was named Wentworth, a crack shot and a fine hunter. He was the hero of one of Ned Buntline's stories and Buntline called him the Little White Whirlwind. After North had satisfied himself that there were not more than twenty-five or thirty warriors in the approaching group, he started back towards the command and soon overtook Wentworth, whose horse was slow. He asked Luther to stay with him and was told that as the command was but a short distance behind and the other two soldiers would soon meet them, there was not much danger. Even if the Indians did overtake them, they could hold them off until the troops came.

At a deep ravine on Dry creek that ran into the north Loup, they stopped, thinking that this would be a good place to put up a fight. North left his horse in the ravine and climbed back up the bank to wait for the Indians. He could see on top of a high hill three or four Indians who had crossed the river near their camp. They probably could see the troops, for one of them began to ride his horse in a circle and to wave his blanket at the same time. He was probably signaling to the Indians that were following Luther North. These all stopped and after talking a little turned and rode back and crossed the river and joined the warriors on the hill.

By this time the women had packed their horses and started across the river. North and Wentworth were expecting the troops to appear every minute, but when the women had all passed out of sight behind some hills on the other side of the river, the two white men rode on back to look for the troops. They found them two miles in the rear and dismounted. When the two soldiers had reached the command and reported to Major Switzer about the Indians, he halted and dismounted his men and waited for the coming of the wagons, which were a mile behind. Then he issued one hundred rounds of ammunition to each man. All this took time and gave the Indians a chance to get away. Major Switzer asked Luther what tribe the Indians belonged to and how many there were. North thought it a hunting party of Brule Sioux from the Spotted Tail agency and that there were about one hundred, including women and children.

By this time some of the Indians had ridden up on the hills opposite, on the north side of the river and about a half a mile away and the major told Luther to ride down and tell them to come over, that he wished to talk with them.

He seemed surprised when Luther told him he could not talk the Sioux language, but would try to make them understand. Luther and Wentworth went down to the river and motioned for them and six or seven came across. One of them knew a few words of English and when asked what they wanted he said, "Sugar, coffee and flour." Major Switzer made a speech to them that they could not in the least understand, telling them they must go home and be good Indians and gave them sugar, coffee and hardtack. They went away rejoicing and that was the last seen of them. A few days later the military camp on the north Loup was reached.

While in camp Luther North devoted much of his time to hunting, and furnished meat for the infantry company, while Wentworth did most of the hunting for the cavalry company. One morning North had started out a little after sunrise with a couple of soldiers and one of the teamsters with a wagon, to get a load of elk meat and when ten miles from camp a messenger from Major Switzer overtook him, with orders to return to camp. When he got there Major Switzer told him he had some dispatches to send to Grand Island and said that Luther was to take them and get the answer and return to camp as soon as possible.

North left the camp at eleven o'clock and a lieutenant and twenty-five men were sent to ride with him for the first twenty miles, since Major Switzer had heard that the country was full of Indians. It was sixty miles to Grand Island and after the soldiers turned back at the end of twenty miles, he rode the rest of the way alone. He saw no Indians, but crossed the trail of a war party of perhaps fifty mounted Indians, so fresh that where they had crossed the creek the bank was still wet where the water had splashed as the horses climbed out He left the traveled road and kept in the ravines as much as possible, crossed the south Loup a little west of St. Paul, and reached Grand Island before seven o'clock. He had ridden that day eighty miles in all. He took his horse to a livery barn and had him fed and given a good rubdown. Then he took the despatches to the telegraph office and had some supper. In about an hour the answers came and at nine o'clock he saddled his horse and started back.

Just after crossing the south Loup at St. Paul, he was caught in a terrific thunderstorm and the wind blew so hard and it was so dark that he had to turn his back to it and wait until it was over. Then he started on and at a little before four o'clock was at the camp, having ridden one hundred and forty miles in twenty hours on one horse, the best he ever owned. Pretty much all this ride was made on a trot, though occasionally he would break into a canter for a mile or two. The wild west pictures of scouts dashing madly off on a gallop for a long ride are not faithful. A scout starting on a long ride had to be as careful as possible of his horse and keep him in as good condition as he could, so that if he had to make a run for it, his horse was ready.

After taking care of his horse, Luther delivered his package to the major's orderly, and went to his tent to get something to eat. He was drinking some coffee when Major Switzer sent for him. When Luther reached his tent, the major said, I am very much surprised to see you back so soon, how do you feel? He told him that he was all right and the major said, I hate to ask you to start out again now, but I must send someone down to St. Paul at once. If you will furnish me with a horse, I will go, was the answer. The quartermaster furnished a horse and in a few minutes North was again on his way and before eleven o'clock was back at St. Paul, where he was to stay until the next day.

Of the rest of this ride and his service as scout with Major Switzer, Captain North has written thus:

"The weather was pretty warm and about three o'clock I took my blanket and went out on the east side of the house, and thought I would take a nap before supper. I had ridden one hundred eighty miles, and had gone without sleep for nearly thirty-six hours, as I had gotten up about four o'clock the morning before. I went to sleep and the next I knew the lady of the house was calling me and the sun was shining in my face. It was morning and she was calling me to breakfast. She said she had come to call me for supper the night before, but I was sleeping so soundly she hated to wake me up. It was after six o'clock and I had slept for fifteen hours straight. I ate my breakfast and afterward went out into the hills and killed an antelope.

"Shortly after I got back, the mail carrier came in from Grand Island and I got the mail for the camp and that afternoon started back. About fifteen miles out, I saw some horse tracks crossing the road and followed them for four or five miles, when I came in sight of some Indians. There were eight of them, and as I wanted to know whether they were Sioux or Pawnees, I rode down in a canyon that ran parallel to the course, they were taking, and by riding pretty fast I managed to get ahead of them. When I got to the head of the ravine, I fastened my horse and crept up to the top of the bank. They were about a quarter of a mile away, and through my glasses I could see that they were Pawnees. I then stood up and shouted to them, and they came over. I saw they were surprised to see me. They told me a party of Sioux had been down to the Pawnee agency and stolen a lot of horses, and they had followed them, but had given up hope of overtaking them and were now on their way home. I told them of the trail I had crossed two days before, and they said that was the party they were after. We sat down on the hill and smoked and talked for a half hour or so, when they started for home. I went on to camp, where I arrived about sundown.

"I told Major Switzer about meeting the Pawnees and he said, 'If you run across anymore of them in this country, tell them to go back to their reservation and stay there; that any Indians found away from their reservation will be considered hostile, and will be treated as such.' I thought of telling him that if he treated all the hostiles as he did the party of Sioux we had met a short time before, by giving them sugar, coffee and hardtack, they would all be hostile, but I kept still.

"While I was in this camp we caught five young elk, and raised them on a bottle. Captain Munson had a pair of them broken to drive, and I believe later took them to Omaha, where he drove them through the streets, but they caused several teams to run away, and he gave up driving them.

"The latter part of June we started out on a scout with the cavalry company, and after going up the north Loup one day, we crossed over to the Cedar river and marched down it, and after lying in camp one day, the major asked me if we could cross the country from there to our camp in one day. I told him we could, but that the country was pretty rough on wagons, and the trail would not be very straight. He said we would try it, so we started the next morning and traveled until noon, when we came to some water-holes, where we camped for dinner. After eating we started on, and when over within a few miles of the Loup river we got into the rough hills, and I had to zigzag back and forth among the heads of the canyons to find a road for the wagons. Two or three times the major had said to me, Can't you find a straighter road than this? I tried to explain to him that as soon as I could get down off the hills we were following on to the little stream to our right, we would follow the valley of the creek right down to the river, and would be just opposite our camp, and that the road would be good all the way. Finally, as I was making another turn, around the head of a canyon he said, I think if we went off to the left here, we would find a much straighter and better road;

I said to him, If you know so much about this country you don't need a guide; and I started off on a gallop and was soon out of sight.

"In an hour I was in camp and went to the quartermaster and told him I was through. He settled with me and then said, Could not you and the old man get along together? When I told him what had happened he was very much amused, and said, It is a wonder he didn't put you under arrest. I said, He did not have time, as I left suddenly. He then asked me when the command would get to camp. I told him if they kept on in the direction they were going when I left them, they would never get to camp with the wagons, as they were heading for some canyons; that they would never get them out. This proved to be the case, for the major arrived at a canyon where he could go no further, and in trying to turn back, one of the wagons rolled over into the canyon and was completely demolished, and they abandoned it. The command finally made a dry camp and came in the next day. I had gone down the river a few miles and stopped with a settler friend of mine, and it was a couple of months before I was in that part of the country again."

A week or two after this Luther North started back to Columbus. Three or four miles down the river from Spring creek he came upon the ruins of an old Pawnee village and could plainly see the walls of some of their earth houses. He dismounted and walked through the village and presently came to a great circle, the outline of a building that was seventy yards in diameter. This puzzled him, for he had never seen nor heard of a house so large. When he reached the Pawnee village that day, he saw Eagle Chief, the chief of the Skiri, and asked him about it. Eagle Chief said that the Skiri had lived at that place a long time ago and that the big lodge was probably a general meeting place and was used for all public gatherings, councils and religious ceremonies. He said also that it was while living at that village that the Skiri became separated.

They were going on their summer hunt and part of them started ahead of the others. These went north, probably as far as the Niobrara, when they were attacked by Sioux and were defeated and as the Sioux were to the south of them-that is between them and their own people they retreated to the north until they came to the

134

Missouri river. They followed up the Missouri until they met the Mandan Indians, with whom they made a treaty. They built houses there and have lived near or with the Mandans ever since. They are called the Arikara.

Luther had supper with Eagle Chief and they sat up talking until nearly morning. The chief said that before this separation the Skiri were a very large tribe and could hold their own with any of their enemies, but after that they had rather a hard time and at last were conquered by the Lak tats led i hu the Tsau i, the Kit ka hak and the Pita hau i rat, later known as the lower village tribes. That was a long time after the separation of the Skiri.

Several writers tell of the return of the Arikaras in 1833, and say they lived with the Skiri for two or three years but that they were so quarrelsome and dirty that the Skiri drove them away, and they went back to the Mandans. Eagle Chief must have been past twenty years old in 1833 and he declared quite positively to Luther North that the Arikara had never come back. Some of them had been back to visit the Skiri, but it is altogether unlikely that they ever came back as a tribe, or that perhaps more than a dozen ever came at one time.

In the autumn of 1873 Luther North headed a party that was engaged in collecting vertebrate fossils for Professor O. C. Marsh of Peabody museum of Yale college. He had four men with him and worked in the Pawnee Butte country east of Greeley, Colorado, for some months with good success. Returning to his home he spent the winter in Columbus.

CHAPTER XVIII

In the spring of 1874, General George A. Custer, lieutenant-colonel of the Seventh cavalry, was ordered to explore the Black Hills country then scarcely known. He invited me to go along in a scientific capacity and I asked Luther North to go with me as an assistant.

The expedition started from Fort Abraham Lincoln, Dakota, which was not far from Bismarck, but on the west side of the Missouri river. The military command included six troops of the Seventh cavalry and two companies of infantry under Major Tilford. Colonel William Ludlow, chief engineer of the department of Dakota, Colonel George A. Forsyth* and Colonel Fred D. Grant [son of then President Ulysses S. Grant], aides on General Sheridan's staff, were with us, as well as a number of civilians, a so-called scientific staff among whom were Professors Donaldson and N. K. Winchell of Minnesota several newspaper men, a photographer, two miners and a number of Indian scouts from the Santee Sioux and the Arikara Indians. The whole company must have numbered nearly 1200 men.

George Alexander "Sandy" Forsyth (1837–1915) was a career military officer and veteran of the Civil War. In September, 1868, he led a force that engaged bands led by Roman Nose in the Battle of Beecher Island.—Ed. 2015

While Luther North and I were waiting for the boat at Bismarck, then the end of the Northern Pacific railroad track, some Indians standing near us began to talk among themselves and Luther North recognized that they were speaking a language that sounded like Pawnee. He spoke to one of them in Pawnee, asking if he could understand him. The Indian said he understood and at once began to talk to North. These were Arikaras, speaking the language used by the Skiri band of Pawnees. They could understand North very well, but their dialect differed somewhat from that of the Skiri, so that he could not always readily make out what they were saying. These were some of the scouts who were going on the expedition with Custer. Two years later, their leader, Bloody Knife,* was killed with Custer.

Bloody Knife was Custer's favorite Arikara scout and was killed during the Valley Fight at Little Bighorn on June 25, 1876. He was seated on his horse next to Major Marcus Reno, who had just asked him a question. Bloody Knife was hit by a bullet in the head, splatting his blood and brains in the face of Reno.—Ed. 2015

At Fort Lincoln the expedition was detained about thirty days and then started for the Black Hills. As it left the fort a band of sixteen men mounted on white horses preceded it, playing Garry Owen, Custer's favorite air. To start into a supposedly hostile Indian country accompanied by a brass band was a novel experience to some of those who rode with this expedition.

The trip into the hills was interesting and many of the people on the expedition were worth talking to. Colonel Ludlow was a great man in ability, force and charm. Colonel Forsyth had been in command of the scouts that fought with the Cheyennes on the Arikara Fork of the Republican river in 1868. This is usually spoken of as the battle of Beecher's island, because Lieutenant Beecher was killed in the fight. There too was killed the famous Cheyenne brave, Roman Nose. Forsyth was wounded the first day, having his leg badly broken. They were surrounded for nine days before relief came from Fort Wallace. Colonel Forsyth was a very interesting talker and a man of great determination.

General Custer was friendly, sociable and agreeable. He was very fond of hunting and a great believer in his skill as a rifle shot. He had with him a pack of greyhounds and scotch deer hounds that he thought very highly of and which he told everyone had overtaken and killed many antelope. They did nothing of this kind on the Black Hills expedition and, though they chased antelope frequently, they never caught any. They did kill plenty of jack rabbits.

On the plains General Custer did no shooting that was notable. It was observed that, though he enjoyed telling of the remarkable shots that he himself commonly made, he did not seem greatly interested in the shooting done by other people. On one occasion when Luther North and I were traveling not far from the command, three deer frightened by its passage, ran by us and North killed the three with three successive shots. That day when we reached camp, I took the saddle of one of the deer over to the general's tent and when I gave it to him, said, "Captain North did some remarkable shooting today. He killed three running deer in three shots." Custer's response to this remark was, "Huh, I found two more horned toads today."

As we were returning to Fort Lincoln and were crossing the Bad Lands of the Missouri, while riding with General Custer ahead of the command we came to a small pond, near which a duck had nested. Seven or eight half grown young ones were swimming about and General Custer got off his horse and said, "I will knock the heads off a few of them."

I looked at Luther North and made a sign to him and he dismounted and sat down on the ground behind the general. General Custer fired at a bird and missed it and North shot and cut the head off one of the birds. Custer shot again and missed and North cut the head off another bird. Custer looked around at him and then shot again and again missed and North cut the head off a third duck.

Just then an officer rode up over a hill near the pond and said that the bullets after skipping off the water were singing over the heads of his troops. The general said "We had better stop shooting"; and mounted the horse and rode on without saying a word.

The hills proved to be a good hunting country; deer, elk, and bears, were plentiful. There were some big horn and smaller game was abundant. There were also some mountain lions. One day General Custer killed a very large grizzly, a battle scarred veteran. The general distributed the meat freely to different messes, but probably little of it was eaten, for it was an aged animal, very tough and very strong.

On the return trip, soon after crossing the Little Missouri river, the abandoned camp was found of a great body of Indians. In conversation that evening in front of General Custer's tent, Luther North remarked that perhaps it was just as well the Indians had gone before the expedition got there, as there were a great many of them. Custer commented "I could whip all the Indians in the northwest with the Seventh cavalry." Perhaps he felt in that way when he found the villages on the Little Big Horn two years later. He considered the Indians very inferior fighters and when he charged the village on the Little Big Horn he undoubtedly thought that he would win a great victory. He was a good soldier and a good fighter, but like most white men he did not understand Indians and underrated them.

It may be doubted if any braver men ever lived than the Cheyenne and Pawnee Indians. The Cheyennes have often been defeated, but usually when fighting with bows and arrows against men armed with breech loading firearms. The Pawnees, who defeated the Cheyennes at Plum creek under Frank North were somewhat disciplined and fought as a unit; while the Cheyennes fought, as in fact all Indians fought, each man for himself.

Much has been written about the great chiefs, Sitting Bull, Red Cloud, Spotted Tail, Crazy Horse and American Horse, of the Sioux, and Tall Bull, Dull Knife and Roman Nose of the Cheyennes. They have been described as great leaders and in a fashion this is true. Besides being themselves brave, these men were orators, able to stir the emotions and were looked up to with much respect. Some of them were great warriors, but in battle not one of them could have given an order that would have been obeyed, for among the Indians there was no such thing as discipline. If some great warrior wished to charge the enemy, he would say "Now, I am going" and, if a group of young men felt disposed to do so they would follow him. But if Red Cloud or Sitting Bull had picked out two or three hundred men and ordered them to charge the enemy in a body no attention would have been paid to the order. The individual Indian fought just in his own way and took orders from no one and it was for this reason that Indians so seldom conquered disciplined troops. The Cheyenne chief known as Old Little Wolf, however, gave orders to his men and enforced them.

The expedition reached Fort Lincoln on its return about the first of September and from St. Paul, Minnesota, Luther North went to Columbus, to find all Nebraska eaten up by the grasshoppers.

In the summer of 1876 just after the Little Big Horn fight and the killing of General Custer, Major North urged to it by the persuasion of his neighbors and some old frontiersmen telegraphed General Sherman offering to raise a volunteer regiment to take field against hostile Indians. He was advised that there was no law authorizing such action, but soon after this he was ordered to report to General Sheridan in Chicago, and asked to go to the Indian territory and enlist one hundred Pawnee scouts. Major North was to be captain of this company and was to have two other white officers. The scouts were to furnish their own horses and after being mustered in were to be taken to Sidney barracks.

General Sheridan, who some time before had been at the Wichita agency, at a time when many Pawnees were there with the Wichitas, insisted that the Pawnees were established there and that it was to the Wichita agency that Major North should go to enlist his scouts. Major North knew very well that the Pawnees were not there, but General Sheridan believed that he knew better. Major North and his brother Luther went to the Wichita agency as directed and there were informed that-as they already knew, the Pawnees had been moved to their new agency one hundred and eighty miles north. They were therefore obliged to return to the railroad and to go to the Pawnee agency which meant a ride of 125 miles from Coffeyville to the Pawnee agency.

The morning after their arrival Major North called a council of the Pawnee chiefs and asked their permission to enlist their young men as scouts, to the number of one hundred. Practically every man in the tribe wanted to go, but only one hundred could be taken. After their removal to this new country in the south almost all the horses owned by the Pawnees had died and Major North was obliged to march the enlisted men on foot to Coffeyville, there telegraphing to General Sheridan that it would be necessary to furnish horses for the scouts. North had determined that if General Sheridan could not furnish horses he would send the scouts he had enlisted back to their reservation.

Major North and the enlisted men were followed to the railroad station of Coffeyville by many young men of the tribe, who apparently hoped that Major North would finally take them along, or that some of those already chosen would drop out and leave vacancies to be filled. None dropped out, however, and when Major North put the enlisted Indians on the train, he was obliged to station guards to keep other Pawnees who wished to go along from getting on the cars.

The eagerness to enlist felt by the Pawnees was in part due to the fact that they had been reduced by sickness to abject poverty and were in deplorable condition. They were then poorer than Major North had ever before seen them. They had no blankets to wear, and their food was scanty and of poor quality. It is not surprising that they all wished to go out on the warpath against the Sioux and to receive from the government, abundant rations, warm uniforms and fair pay.

When the men enlisted got beyond Omaha on their way north, they became greatly excited by the approach to their old home. They were wild with joy and pointed out to one another the different points along the Platte river where they used to live. They sang and danced and told stories of war parties and buffalo hunts. When they reached Fremont they pointed out the hill called Pah huk, which they believed was the place where the na-hu-rak (spirit animals) live. This hill is on the bank of the Platte river, and the cut bank below it is perhaps two hundred feet high and perpendicular, and in those days the water beneath it was quite deep. The entrance to the spirit house was thought to be under the water and those Pawnees who said they had been in the house, or lodge, declared that they had been guided into it by a little bird. Following this little bird they jumped off the bank into the water, where they found an opening in the bank, a sort of tunnel that led into a lodge. At the end of the tunnel into the lodge were the guards; on one side of the door a large grizzly bear, and on the other side a great rattlesnake. The little bird warned the man he was leading that he must not be afraid, or something terrible would happen to him.

When the young man went in the snake raised his head and rattled loud and threateningly and the grizzly bear stood up on its hind legs and growled fiercely, but the young man made his heart strong and passed be- tween the two as if they were not there and found himself in a great lodge with a fire burning in the center and all the different animals sitting about it. The leader was a great beaver and there were elk and deer, antelope, foxes, coyotes, big wolves and birds. The beaver was the spokesman and welcomed the young man and called him brother. He stayed with them for a time and they taught him how to do many wonderful things. A young man who said he had been in the lodge, could do many things that no one who saw him do them could explain. He was a Pawnee scout in 1869, and was one of their great medicine men. He died soon after the Pawnees moved south in 1874.

Among the men in this company of scouts on its way north was a Ponca Indian, who had married a Pawnee woman and had lived for a long time with the Pawnees. The Pawnee and Poncas had been friends for many years, but there was a time, generations ago, when they had been enemies. After the two tribes had made a treaty of peace, one band of the Pawnees lived on Shell creek, north of the present Schuyler, Nebraska. One day soon after the treaty was made, the Pawnees saw a large band of Ponca warriors coming toward their village. They went out to welcome them, but when they met, the Poncas suddenly threw back their buffalo robes and drew their bows and arrows and began to kill the Pawnees. The Pawnees ran to their lodges, for their arms and, after a desperate battle, which lasted for three days, defeated the Poncas, and drove them back to their home. On their return to the Pawnee village they had a scalp dance and composed a song in commemoration of the victory.

This was such a wonderful victory and the Pawnees liked the song so well that they were still singing it in the middle of the last century and whenever they had a battle and conquered the enemy and had a scalp dance, they would sing that song.

On the way north, after they had come as far as Shell creek, and while the Indians were still talking about their old home, Luther North spoke of the Shell creek village and suggested, "Now let us have the Ponca song." In an instant the talking ceased and not a word was spoken by anyone. North waited for a moment and just as he was about to suggest the song again, one of the head men came over to his seat and said to him, "Father, we have a Ponca with us. It would make him feel badly if we sang that song." This shows the finer feeling of the Indian. It had perhaps been two hundred years since that battle, but now this Ponca was their comrade and they would not do anything to hurt his feelings.

At Sidney, the scouts received arms, uniforms and horses and were mustered into the service to take part in the winter campaign of 1876-1877 under General [George] Crook.* Major North appointed his brother Luther and Lieutenant Cushing as his lieutenants. Luther North and his brother J. E. North purchased at Julesburgh the horses to mount the men. Many cattle were being driven up the trail from Texas that year and with each herd there was a good sized band of cow ponies. There were about three hundred of these nearby and Luther got the hundred he needed in one day.

Crook's force was to approach the Little Bighorn Valley from the south at the same time Custer was approaching from the north up Rosebud Creek. Crook's column was attacked by Crazy Horse and a large Sioux force on June 17, 1876 at the Battle of the Rosebud. Crook had many wounded and was low on ammunition so he withdrew to Goose Creek near present-day Sheridan, Wyoming. Though he reported on this battle to General Sheridan, Generals Terry, Custer, and Gibbon knew nothing about it until after Custer and five companies of his troopers were killed eight days later at the Little Bighorn. Crook's adjutant, Captain John Bourke, wrote one of the best memoirs of this period: On the Border with Crook.—Ed. 2015

On the fifteenth of October, the scouts left Sidney and followed the Sidney and Black Hills stage road until they crossed the Niobrara river, where they went into camp. They had been there only one day when a courier arrived, bringing to Major North orders from the department commander to go to Fort Robinson. The order had evidently been written that morning and its language suggested immediate action for it read "timing your march so as not to show your command near the agency until after dark. A messenger will meet you on the road in order to conduct you to the desired point and you must be here tonight, Sunday, 22."

Major North left his camp about sun-down and started for Fort Robinson on a fast trot. After a ride of fifteen or twenty miles the scouts were met by a lieutenant with a small escort, who brought orders for Major North to join General McKenzie* to assist in the capture of Red Cloud's village. The officer urged Major North to hurry forward rapidly, for the scouts would have to ride forty miles before daylight. Major North explained to him that their horses were not in condition to make such a ride, but said that he could select forty or fifty of the best mounted men who could do it. He therefore chose forty-eight men and horses, and with his brother Luther started off, riding fifteen miles at a sharp trot without stopping and overtook General McKenzie who had with him a detachment of the Fourth cavalry. His scouts were Todd Randall and Louis Richard. North left Lieutenant Cushing behind, with the men whose horses were in poorest condition, to take the baggage wagons on to Fort Robinson.

*Ranald Slidell Mackenzie, also called Bad Hand, (1840–1889) was a career United States Army officer and general in the Union Army during the American Civil War. He was described by General Ulysses S. Grant as its most promising young officer. He badly injured his head in a fall in 1883 and began to exhibit strange behavior. He mustered out of the army in 1884 and declined further until his death.—Ed. 2015

Red Cloud was camped with a group of his people in a village near Chadron creek about forty miles from the Indian agency. The agent, Major Howard, had several times ordered him to come into the agency and to camp near it, but the old chief had not followed his instructions. He gave various reasons, which may or may not have been good. Sometimes he did not answer the orders at all. The agent, however, was afraid that the Indians might break out into hostilities and wanted them nearer to the agency, where the military could perhaps control them. The authorities wished also, in view of the campaign that General Crook was organizing, that all peaceable Indians should be brought together near Fort Robinson. It was in the hope of bringing Red Cloud's camp closer to the agency that General McKenzie had organized this expedition.

CHAPTER XIX

After the Pawnees had joined General McKenzie's force, the command went on for about twenty miles further to a point where the trail forked; for the troops were to go to two Sioux camps, on the same stream. One of these was occupied by Red Cloud and his people, and the other by two lesser chiefs, Yellow Leaf and Swift Bear. Here the cavalry was divided into two detachments of four troops each and with each detachment went twenty-four Pawnee scouts. Major Gordon, commanding one of the parties and Luther North with his Pawnees took the right-hand trail, which led to the camp of Swift Bear. General McKenzie, with the rest of the command, followed the left-hand trail toward Red Cloud's camp.

Major North with some of his Pawnee scouts rode forward well in advance of McKenzie's command, and observed no signs of Indians until after they had gone about five miles, when one of the scouts called Major North's attention to a peculiar sound. They stopped their horses and all listened, and in a few minutes the sound was heard again. It was the crowing of a rooster. North returned to General McKenzie and reported the circumstance, which was explained by Todd Randall who was with the column. He said that they must be close to Red Cloud's camp, for Red Cloud had a lot of chickens. It was now three o'clock in the morning and very dark. Major North again took the lead and the command went forward until they were rather close to the sound. They marched slowly and cautiously and presently came to the top of a cut bank and on the other side of the stream which ran below it, saw Red Cloud's village.

Major North and his scouts looked over the surrounding country and reported to General McKenzie where the troops should be placed. In the two hours that passed before it became light enough for an attack, the troops completely surrounded the village. When the proper time came, General McKenzie ordered Randall to go to the edge of the bank and shout out in the Sioux language that the village was surrounded. This did not cause any general excitement and no men showed themselves, but women and children did come out of the lodge and made an effort to hide in the brush. The Pawnee scouts under orders charged down through the village and rounded up the Indian horses, which were driven to the rear and held there. The cavalrymen now dismounted, marched into the village, where they met with no resistance. The men were secured, disarmed and placed in line under a guard. General McKenzie through his interpreter ordered the women to go to the bunch of horses, choose there enough to carry their baggage and then to break camp as quickly as possible. It was difficult, however, to get these women to do as they were ordered and finally General McKenzie told them that he would give them only a short time longer, and if they did not take down their lodges and pack up their property he would burn the village. This threat may not have been understood by the women; at all events they did nothing, until some of the tents and lodges were actually burning. Then they worked fast enough.

Meantime Major Gordon had surrounded Swift Bear's camp much in the same way as had been done at Red Cloud's. He had given strict orders that not a shot should be fired unless the Indians first fired on the troops. When daylight came, the Pawnee scouts charged through the village and drove all the horses before them. Not a single Indian showed his face outside the lodges until after the Pawnees had passed through the camp and were gathering the loose horses that were feeding on the hill.

After a time the Indians came out and began to talk with Major Gordon and things happened about as they had at Red Cloud's camp. The Indians were finally brought into Camp Robinson; the women and children and the old and feeble riding on the captured horses, but the young men walking.

After Fort Robinson was reached and the men had eaten, Major North took twenty of his scouts and started with the captured horses for Fort Laramie. Many of the men had been in the saddle almost constantly for thirty-four hours, yet they started that night on a ninety-mile ride for Fort Laramie. In the middle of the night, having marched fifty miles, they went into camp for a short rest. About two o'clock in the morning the sentries discovered a rider approaching the camp and halted him until word of his coming was sent to Major North. When he reached the picket line, North found the man was a messenger from General Crook with dispatches for Fort Laramie, the nearest telegraph station. The messenger said that he had left Fort Robinson at ten o'clock that night and had ridden the fifty miles in four hours; that General Crook had held a council with the captured Indians and decided to liberate them, after having deposed Red Cloud from the governmental chieftainship of all the Sioux Indians. The messenger added that it was supposed at the agency that the Indians just liberated would go to the other Indians and secure horses on which to follow Major North, and to recapture from him their own horses. As this seemed rather a natural thing for them to do, Major North ordered his men to saddle up at once and in a few minutes he was again moving towards Fort Laramie, which he reached without adventure and delivered the seven hundred twenty-two head of horses to the quartermaster there. His orders from General McKenzie were, that after turning the horses over to the post quartermaster, he should remain at the post until the rest of the command came.

When Major North reported to the quartermaster that he was ready to turn the horses over to him, that officer replied that he could not care for them, because he had not enough men to herd them. He said however that he would have them put in the corral at night and have them guarded, if during the day Major North would detail men enough to herd them while they were at pasture. This was done for two or three days, but on the second morning when the soldiers turned over the horses to the Pawnees who were to take them out on herd, the Pawnees noticed that some of the horses had disappeared. The same thing was observed the following morning and it appeared that ten or fifteen horses were missing. Major North called upon the quartermaster and inquired whether he would be held responsible for the horses until they were properly disposed of, saying that if so he wished no more guarding to be done by the soldiers, but that he would place his own men over the animals as guards, when he felt sure that no more attempts would be made to steal the stock from the corral. Major North gave orders to the Pawnees to take entire charge of the horses and to kill anyone who tried to take them away. There was no more stealing. It never was learned who the thieves were and the stolen horses were never recovered. Many people wished to get possession of these horses, for among them there were some very good animals. One ranchman even went so far as to try to buy some of the horses from Major North, offering him five hundred dollars for a few of them.

Major North was ordered by General Crook to select one horse for each one of his forty-eight scouts and one for himself and his brother, and to pick out from the remainder two hundred saddle horses to be taken along as extra saddle horses for the scouts. The remainder were afterwards sold at auction.

It was after Frank North had started to Fort Laramie with the horses that Luther North saw California Joe for the last time. California Joe, who had just come down from the Black Hills, was camped only about a mile away. He had been at the Pawnee camp, the night before, and again in the morning, he had come down to see Frank. When he found that Frank North had gone to Laramie, he talked a few minutes with Luther and then went back to his camp, and Luther started for Fort Laramie. After the Pawnees had marched about ten miles, they were overtaken by an infantry lieutenant who was hurrying on to overtake his company. The lieutenant said to Luther, California Joe has just been murdered. Luther replied, I guess that is a mistake. I was talking to him just before we started. The lieutenant said, It was on the way back from your camp to his own that he was killed. Some fellow shot him in the back.

California Joe was a noted scout and guide, a close friend of Wild Bill Hickok and well-known to Jim Bridger and to Carson. He was in Deadwood about the time Wild Bill was murdered and was very outspoken in his views as to the gang of gamblers that he believed responsible for Hickok's death. Some people thought that this same gang caused Joe to be murdered.

For this winter campaign, General Crook had authorized the enlistment of a number of Arapaho, Cheyenne and Sioux scouts. Some of the Sioux were those who had recently been captured in the villages of Red Cloud and Swift Bear. There were about one hundred and twenty of these scouts, all of whom were furnished horses from the two hundred set aside as a reserve by General Crook. The Sioux,

148

who knew the horses, were permitted to select those for the scouts and very naturally chose the best ones, leaving only a small herd of the poorest for Major North to handle. He finally, with General Crook's consent, turned over this remainder to the Sioux scouts.

The horse Major North had selected for himself was a splendid bay, said to be the swiftest runner of all the horses in the Sioux nation. He had belonged to Three Bears and was his favorite war-horse. While Major North was still holding the two hundred horses before he had suggested that they be turned over to the Sioux Three Bears, accompanied by Lieutenant Clark, came to him and presented an order for a horse from General Crook. Major North sent a corporal with Lieutenant Clark and Three Bears to the herd, but the old chief did not find there the animal, which he wished to recover on the order. Lieutenant Clark then told the corporal to take them to the private herd, and there Three Bears found his favorite steed. The horse recognized him at once and came up to him. Three Bears put a rope around his neck and was about to lead him away, notwithstanding the vigorous protest of the corporal, who insisted that the animal was the property of Major North. Three Bears and Lieutenant Clark went with the horse to the camp of Major North. When North saw the animal in the possession of the Sioux chief he was indignant. He walked to the horse and threw the rope off his neck and put his own lariat around the horse's neck and tied him to a stake near his tent door, saying, That horse is mine and I propose to keep him. You can't take him. The Indians have been trying to get him long enough.

I'll report this matter to General Crook, said Lieutenant Clark, And I think we'll have a redistribution of these horses.

You may redistribute them, replied Major North, but you'll not get this horse.

Lieutenant Clark and Three Bears rode away and Major North and his brother at once mounted the horses given them by General Crook and rode up to headquarters. They found Lieutenant Clark, and all went to see the general, where the case was laid before him. He told Lieutenant Clark that before trying to get the horse for Three Bears he should have gone to Major North and learned from

149

him how the horses had been distributed. Then addressing Major North:

You need not worry about this matter, said General Crook, All the horses which I gave to you and your command shall be retained by you and the right to hold them shall not be questioned.

Major North returned to his quarters feeling easier, but for the next few days and nights the Sioux were observed to be continually lurking about the herd of horses, perhaps looking for an opportunity to recapture Three Bears' horse, which Major North always kept tied close to his tent door to prevent its being stolen. The Major finally became satisfied that sooner or later they would get the horse, and sold him to a white scout, who took him to the Shoshoni agency in the Wind River mountains, where he soon won the reputation of being the fastest runner in that section of the country.

The gray horse which had been assigned to Lieutenant North was given the name of Swift Bear, and he also proved to be a very fleet runner.

By the fifteenth of November, everything was in readiness for the winter campaign and the little army, consisting of two thousand troops, infantry and cavalry, all under command of General Crook, moved out and marched to Fort Fetterman, where they remained for about a week. One day while here, General Crook said to Major North, The Sioux and Cheyennes scouts are complaining to me that your Pawnees are keeping themselves too distant and cool and that they will not come near them nor associate with them in any way. They say that as they are soldiers now, they would like to be friends with the Pawnees.

To make them friends, general, said Major North, Will be very difficult for they have been bitterest enemies for many years. A fierce hatred has existed between them for generations. Then he related to the general the history of their enmity. Now, general, if you wish to issue an order commanding the Pawnees to make up with their bitterest enemies, said the major, I will do all in my power to have it obeyed.

No, I don't wish to force them to be friendly against their will. Yet if they were friendly, I believe it would be better for all concerned, said General Crook.

Well, I'll talk to my Pawnees about it and hear what they have to say, replied the major.

The Pawnees, however, were not inclined to respond to friendly advances. They said that the Sioux had no more love for them than they had for the Sioux and that the Sioux were merely making a pretense of wishing to become friends so that they might have a better opportunity of getting their captive horses back from the Pawnees.

The command moved on to Fort Reno, on Powder river, where it was joined by about one hundred Shoshoni scouts, under Tom Cosgrove. The chief of these Shoshoni was the son of old Washaki.

At this point the Sioux again complained to General Crook of their continued cool treatment by the Pawnees and the general accordingly held a council in order, if possible, to adjust the matter. There were present at this council the Cheyennes, the Sioux, the Shoshoni and the Pawnees. The general talked to them and impressed upon their minds the importance of being friends, temporarily at least, since they must move along together in the command and possibly engage in battle side by side, where united action was necessary.

In starting out on the campaign the Indians had all been supplied with uniforms and at the council the Pawnees appeared in full uniform, but some of the Sioux and Cheyennes attended in native war dress. Major North and Tom Cosgrove noticed this and called it to the attention of General Crook. They said to him that these Indians ought not to be allowed in the council, which had been called for the purpose of creating a better feeling among the scouts. General Crook seemed to pay but little attention to the matter, except that in continuing his remarks to the Indians, he said, "You, as well as ourselves, are servants of the Great Father at Washington and we all ought to dress in the uniform of the soldier and for the time being we all ought to be brothers."

Some of the Indians arose and made speeches, saying that they understood the object of the council and that they intended to act in accordance with the general's wishes and be brothers. Three Bears arose and walking across the circle to the Pawnees, shook hands with Frank White, one of their sergeants, and then presenting him with a horse, said, "Brother, we want to be friends and as an evidence of my sincerity I give you this horse." White accepted the gift and returned his thanks in a very graceful manner, adding that he, too, desired to be friendly.

It was a somewhat affecting scene, and had some influence in lessening the feeling between the Pawnees and Sioux. The council was then dismissed and the Indians dispersed and from that time on, more amicable relations existed among all the Indian scouts, particularly between the Pawnees and the Shoshoni-a tribe related to the Comanches who had not before met the Pawnees. The Pawnees having recently come up from the Indian territory where the Comanches were living, gave to the Shoshoni much interesting information concerning the latter.

From Fort Reno the command marched to Crazy Woman's Fork, where they were to go into camp for several days. At this point it was expected to meet some Sioux scouts that General Crook had sent into the Powder river country to ascertain, if possible, the location of Crazy Horse and his party. Sooq after the command was settled in camp, General Crook decided to send a scouting party into the Big Horn mountains, and ordered out General McKenzie with eight hundred troops, together with nearly all the Indian scouts the Pawnees, Sioux, Arapahoes, Cheyennes and Shoshoni. Major North, with his brother, took about seventy of the Pawnees, leaving Lieutenant Cushing with the remainder in charge of the company property.

On the first day out, General McKenzie marched to Powder river, a distance of twenty miles and there at night sent out two Arapaho and two Sioux scouts to explore the mountains for Indians, as well as to find a route of march for the next day. At eight o'clock the next morning, the command moved over the country towards the mountains and at noon, two of the scouts, who had been out all

152

night, returned and reported to General McKenzie that they had found an Indian village on a tributary of the Powder river, and said that to avoid discovery it would be advisable for the troops to march no further that day, but to keep out of sight as much as possible until dark, and then resume the march on the village. General McKenzie, acting upon this information, moved his men into a deep cañon, at the foot of the mountain, and remained there all the afternoon.

When night came the march was resumed and was kept up all night over a very rough country. They frequently had to go through deep ravines or cañons, so narrow that it was impossible for more than one horse to pass through at a time, and the troops had to string out in single file. After passing through a cañon the troops galloped up together again, and formed in columns of fours. It was a very tiresome march, and the men looked forward to the approach of daylight? Just before the break of day they heard, in the distance, the monotonous beating of Indian drums and then singing and shouting and war-whoops. The Indians were having a scalp dance and had kept it up all through the night. It was to celebrate a successful raid which they had made into the Wind river mountains, where they had killed a party of nine Shoshoni Indians, who were hunting buffaloes. It was learned that the village consisted of one hundred and eighty lodges, or about fourteen hundred persons, among whom were four hundred warriors, and that they were Cheyennes, under command of the famous chiefs, Dull Knife and old Little Wolf. The Indians were located in a large valley which could be entered by cavalry at only one point, an opening through which a creek passed.

General McKenzie halted the command and summoning the company commanders, he gave them his orders for the plan of attack. Major North, with his Pawnee scouts and the Shoshoni, moved along the left bank of the creek as ordered. General McKenzie, with the remainder of the command, marched up the opposite side of the stream. The route was a difficult one, particularly on the left bank, where Major North was marching. The mountain was very steep and the trail ran along the mountain side as if on a terrace.

153

The men and horses were obliged to move very cautiously, for if a horse missed his footing, he would fall down over a precipice two or three hundred feet high to be dashed to pieces at the bottom. The troops passed through this small opening in the mountains with great difficulty and emerged upon the edge of the pocket and suddenly saw before them, in the open plain, the Indian village distant perhaps three-quarters of a mile.

CHAPTER XX

General McKenzie ordered his bugler to sound the charge and as the notes of the bugle rang out loud and clear, the whole command dashed at full gallop towards the village. Major North charged along the cañon side, while General McKenzie led his cavalry up the opposite bank of the creek. When within a few hundred yards of the village one of the Pawnee scouts, who had been assigned to duty with General McKenzie, shouted to Major North that General McKenzie wished him to cross the stream with his command. The opportunity for a brilliant and effective dash on the village was checked. As soon as North reached a point where he could cross, however, he turned and the scouts followed him over the stream. This was deep and miry and in crossing twenty-five or thirty horses were stuck in the mud. They finally got over and joined the command with General McKenzie.

The delay in getting the mired Pawnee horses out of the mud had given some of the Cheyennes time to get away from their camp and to hurry most of their people up among the rocks, where they were safe from the charging troops. Nevertheless, the charge on the village was made with spirit.

Just as the Pawnees were near the village, Frank and Luther North riding at their head, a man rose from the willows very near to Luther, but to his right and threw up his gun on him. He saw the Indian as he rose, twisted in the saddle and shot to his right. The two reports sounded as one and the Pawnees passed on. After the fight, when some of the Pawnees returned, they found the man dead. He was said to be a son of Dull Knife, one of the three sons of that chief who were killed that day.

The Indians had been dancing all night and many of them were now sleeping. Upon hearing the shouts of the approaching scouts, the shots and the drumming of the horses hoofs, they sprang from their sleep and ran out of their lodges, only to see the troops close upon them. The warriors instantly broke and ran pell-mell for the mountains, not having time to reach their horses, which they were compelled to leave behind. The Pawnees on the dash through the

155

village killed five or six of the Cheyennes and scattered the fugitives, who fled up the mountains, retreating slowly behind their women and children and fighting from every bit of cover. In the effort to drive some Cheyennes out of a ravine, Lieutenant McKinney of the Fourth cavalry and some of his men were killed. At last, the Cheyennes got their families up the almost perpendicular mountain side where they built breastworks and held the soldiers back. After they had accomplished this, the warriors continued to fight and tried to work closer to the troops to make their fire more effective. A hot fight was kept up all day without intermission.

During the whole fight General McKenzie conducted himself with great bravery, constantly exposing himself to the fire of the enemy by riding over the open field of battle from one portion of his command to another, giving his orders with entire coolness. While he was crossing the open plain from the main command to a detachment about five hundred yards distant, the full fire of the Indians was directed at him, but he was not hit. Just after this, he sent orders to Major North and Lieutenant North to report to him at once and in galloping across this same open space, they received two or three volleys from the Indians, but escaped injury. Soon afterwards two soldiers attempted to make the same trip on foot, but both were hit, one being killed and the other wounded.

During the battle a small group of Cheyennes hidden among some rocks were firing constantly at a hill where the wounded troops had been brought together. General McKenzie asked Major North if he thought it possible to drive these men from their hiding place, and North said he would try. He blew a call on his whistle and presently half a dozen Pawnees with a non-commissioned officer came to him and he gave some orders. The Pawnees stripped off their uniforms and boots, put on moccasins and tying handkerchiefs about their heads so that they should not be mistaken for hostiles, set off up the mountainside. Not long after, the firing from these rocks ceased and it was later reported that the Pawnees had driven out these Cheyennes, after killing one or two of them.

In the valley, just under the ridge where the Cheyennes were intrenched, was a band of ninety or one hundred of their horses, and four or five of the Arapaho scouts made a dash to try to capture them, but were driven back. A few minutes later, some of the Shoshoni scouts tried it. They failed, and one of them was shot through the body. Three Bears of the Sioux scouts and three of his men, then tried to get around and drive off the horses, and they also returned without them. Just as soon as a party started for the horses, the Cheyennes concentrated their fire on it. Each of the parties that tried and failed was jeered at on its return by the other scouts. After Three Bears' attempt, Luther North asked his brother to let him try for them. Frank did not want him to go, but Luther said, All the other scouts have tried it, why shouldn't the Pawnees? Frank replied, If the Pawnees try it, I shall expect them to bring in the horses. How many men do you want? Luther said one would be enough and he chose a man that had been in his company for three years. His Pawnee name was Pi-isk-i-le-shar, Boy Chief, but he had taken a white man's name, Pete Headman.

The creek came down past the ridge within a hundred yards of where the horses were feeding, and along the stream grew a clump of quaking aspen. The two men got behind that and followed up the stream. Each carried a blanket over his arm and they had their revolvers, but had left their rifles behind. When they had come as near to the horse herd as they could without being seen, they rode out of the brush on a run, and as they reached the horses shook their blankets and yelled at them. The horses were scattered over much ground and were not very easily frightened, but finally were gotten together and driven down through the village and across the creek and behind the butte where the Pawnees were. The Cheyennes were shooting at them constantly and three or four of the horses were killed, but Luther North and Pete Headman came through untouched. A few days afterward General McKenzie gave the Pawnee scouts the whole bunch of horses to be divided among them.

The fighting ceased when darkness came. The loss to General McKenzie's command was: Lieutenant McKinney and six soldiers killed and seventeen wounded. The Cheyennes lost about twenty killed.

The lodges in the abandoned village were still standing, and fearing that during the night the Indians might make a dash with the hope of securing some of their supplies, General McKenzie located his camp in such a position as to cover the village, while Major North and his Pawnees camped in the centre of it. The Indians fired occasional shot at the village, but more or less at random, until some of the Pawnees built a fire to cook some buffalo meat, of which large quantities were found in the lodges. The fire made a bright light and now the Cheyennes had something to shoot at.

Their bullets struck close to the fire, scattering the dirt in every direction and sending some of it into the frying pans. The Pawnees were very hungry, having had nothing to eat all day, and notwithstanding the bullets they continued to prepare their meat, which was soon ready. When they sat down to eat, however, the Cheyennes opened fire on them with more vigor than ever, and succeeded in killing a mule that stood just beyond the fire. The Cheyennes were firing, at very long range, but they had a heavy gun which sent its balls close to the fire. Major North saw that they would probably continue firing all night. He accordingly had breastworks thrown up of the bundles of dried buffalo meat. Behind these the Pawnees found themselves safe from the shots of the enemy and there they lay down to rest in security.

During the night a heavy snow storm began and by morning the ground was covered with five or six inches of snow, which continued to fall. General McKenzie ordered the village destroyed. The lodges were fired and soon everything was burned up. It was a very rich village, over one thousand saddles were destroyed, together with a great number of buffalo robes and a large quantity of buffalo meat. It was impossible to reach the Cheyennes in their mountain fastnesses and General McKenzie gave orders to prepare for the return march to General Crook's camp on Crazy Woman's Fork. Travois were made in sufficient number to carry the dead and wounded. This work was assigned to Lieutenant Homer W. Wheeler who carried it through with singular skill and success.

At noon the captured horses, about six hundred and fifty, were gathered together and the command started on the return trip.

Because of the heavy snow and the difficulties of the transportation of the wounded men, this was a slow hard march. The wounded suffered greatly and one of them died. On the fifth day General McKenzie ordered the captured horses distributed among the Indian scouts. The Pawnees were given sixty of the horses and were satisfied. Four horses each were given to the two Sioux and the two Arapaho scouts who had discovered the Cheyenne village. They were allowed to make their own selection. Three Bears was given two horses, Frank White of the Pawnees and Dick Lushbaugh each received two and in several other instances, deeds of exceptional bravery were rewarded by the presentation of an extra horse.

The next day, the command reached General Crook's camp. General Crook was greatly pleased with the result of the expedition, and highly complimented General McKenzie and his command.

The defeated Cheyennes went to Clear creek, down that to lake De Smet, then to Prairie Dog creek, to Tongue river, to Otter creek and to Beaver creek where they found the Sioux who treated them kindly.

On the same day that they returned to the camp, Major North under instructions from General Crook, sent out his brother, Lieutenant North with four Pawnees, to discover, if possible, the Cheyenne trail. It was bitter cold. They started at eight o'clock in the evening and reached Clear creek before daylight but could find no trail, the snow which was eighteen inches deep, having drifted and covered up every track.

The troops supposed that the command would move from there towards the Tongue river, but the next morning they started back to Fort Reno, where the remains of Lieutenant McKinney and the soldiers killed by the Cheyennes were buried and the wounded men were placed in the hospital. Here, the Shoshoni left the command and returned to their reservation in the Wind river country.

The command remained a day at Fort Reno and then moved to the Dry Fork of the Powder river and stayed a few days. The next move was to the northeast, towards Pumpkin Buttes. Upon reaching the

Belle Fourche river, they marched down that stream about one hundred miles and camped for two weeks.

While in this camp several small parties of miners and prospectors passed by on their way from Dead-wood to the Big Horn mountains. They were informed by the troops of the fight with the Cheyennes in the Big Horn mountains and were warned that some of the Indians might still be there and that it was not safe for them to go there. They went on without paying much attention to the warning. One evening a party of these miners came into camp and they were invited by Major North to spend the night with the scouts and were told of the possibility of meeting Indians. The miners declared that they could whip fifty Indians and declined the invitation and went on and camped five miles further on.

At three o'clock next morning one of the miners unexpectedly came into General Crook's camp and entered the tent of Major North. He was greatly excited and almost exhausted and as soon as he could talk he told Major North that the Indians had attacked the miners' camp about ten o'clock at night and had killed the whole party except himself. He did not know how he had managed to escape. He had no coat or hat and had run the whole distance barefoot over the snow-covered ground and over prickly pear patches. His feet were badly wounded by the prickly pears and were badly frozen. Major North at once had him attended to by some of the scouts, who made him as comfortable as possible. He then reported the case to General Crook, who ordered him to send out a detachment of Pawnees to the miners' camp to investigate the affair and if possible to punish the marauders. The miner was supplied with a pair of large boots, a heavy coat and a hat and was directed to guide Lieutenant North to the camp. The miner stated that he did not think the attacking party consisted of more than four or five Indians. Lieutenant North, who took with him fifteen Pawnees, was instructed to scout the country and after learning in what direction the Indians had gone to return to camp as soon as possible. The scouting party reached the miners' camp before daylight. They found the wagon stripped of everything; all the provisions, arms and ammunition were gone, together with the eleven head of stock. One of the miners was found lying dead in his blanket with his head split open by an axe, which had been placed under his head by the murderers, who, strange as it may seem, had not taken his scalp. No trace of the other three men could be found.

Lieutenant North immediately looked for the trail and presently found it. It looked so fresh that he thought he might possibly overtake the Indians, who would be likely to travel slowly as the horses they had taken were in poor condition. He set out on the trail and followed it for several miles, but finally gave it up. On his way back to camp he met Major North, with twenty scouts, who had come out to look for him, as it was feared he might need assistance, since he had not returned as soon as expected.

General Crook sent a party of men to the miners' camp to bury the dead miner. During the day the three other miners, supposed to have been killed, came into camp one at a time and from different directions. They had had a hard time of it and had wandered about all night long through the snow, but finally all happened to strike General Crook's camp. They had lost everything, and they applied for help to General Crook, who attached them to the command in some capacity, so that they could obtain food. It appeared that the miner who had been killed, had become so frightened by the yelling of the Indians and the suddenness of their attack, that he had covered himself with his blanket and had neither attempted to escape nor offered resistance.

Examination of the miners' camp indicated to Lieutenant North that there were five Indians in the party; some of them barefooted, and that they belonged to the band that had been defeated by General McKenzie. They were in great distress and were out hunting at the time when they struck the miners' camp. They had killed several antelope and were wearing their undressed skins as a protection from the intense cold. They had followed the command in the hope of taking horses.

General Crook now returned to Fort Laramie and on the tenth of January, 1877, the expedition was broken up, most of the troops being ordered to winter quarters at various posts.

Major North with the Pawnees, proceeded to Sidney, making the march in ten days. The Pawnees went into camp at that point. Nothing transpired during their stay there except a sham fight between the Pawnees and a company of the Third cavalry, undertaken for the entertainment of some eastern excursionists, who reached there about the middle of March. The fight was very interesting and at times quite exciting, but terminated rather seriously. Some of the Pawnees were powder marked and burned and several of the horses were severely cut with sabers. One soldier was so badly shot in the face with a blank cartridge that he lost both of his eyes.

While at Camp Robinson, General Crook issued an order, conveying to Major North the expected information that the Pawnee scouts were no longer required and were to be mustered out of the service. General Crook's appreciation of the importance and value of the work performed by Major North and his scouts is expressed in the order which follows:

Headquarters, Department of the Platte, In the Field,

Camp Robinson, Neb., April 19th, 1877 Major Frank North,

Commanding Pawnee Scouts,

Sidney, Nebraska.

Dear Sir: The muster-out of the Pawnee scouts was ordered by Lieutenant-general Sheridan. There is no longer any necessity for the employment of scouts, nor is there any appropriation on hand from which to pay them, for which reasons I regret that I will not be able to retain you in the service.

I think it only just and appropriate to thank you for your excellent behavior during the time of your stay in the military service, under my command, and to say that the soldierlike conduct and discipline of the Pawnee scouts is the most eloquent testimony that could be adduced to prove your fitness for the position you have held as their commanding officer. I remain Very respectfully,

Your obedient servant,

George Crook, Brigadier-general.

The Pawnee scouts were mustered out of the service on the first of May.

This was the end of the organization of the Pawnee battalion. It had performed much useful service and was made up of good men. They were true and loyal soldiers, as brave as anybody of men could be. They were as good trailers as ever lived and thoroughly up to their work as scouts. With a single exception, on every campaign that these scouts made with the troops, it was always the Pawnees that found the hostile Indians and learned where they were situated. This single exception is the case of the Dull Knife village of Cheyennes in November, 1876. This was found by two Arapaho scouts.

Major North, acting under instructions and accompanied by Lieutenant North, now started across the country with the Pawnees to return them to their reservation in the Indian territory. When he had taken them from the territory they were in destitute circumstances, having hardly enough clothing to cover their nakedness and without horses or equipment of any kind. They now returned, comfortably clothed and each one had a good saddle and bridle, purchased out of the money which they had received for their services. They also had fine rifles and pistols and about two hundred fifty horses of their own. Of these one hundred and twenty-five were captured horses and the others they had obtained by trading.

The return trip to the territory occupied thirty days, and was quite a hard journey as the weather was rainy and otherwise disagreeable. Major North who was quite ill, took them nearly to the agency and here they bade him and his brother an affectionate farewell, for they all greatly loved and admired their two commanders. The Norths on their part were deeply sorry to part with the Pawnees.

CONCLUSION

Returning to Nebraska by rail, Major North and his brother were finally mustered out of the United States service on the first day of June (1877).

This was really the first time in fourteen years that Major North had been out of the government service. Owing to almost constant exposure and hardship, his constitution had begun to fail and well knowing that he could no longer endure the trials of campaign service he had already begun to consider finding some business occupation and soon found it.

At the time the Pawnees were mustered out of the service at Sidney, W. F. Cody (Buffalo Bill), who was on his way to San Francisco to fill a theatrical engagement, stopped there to pay Major North a visit. The two had been friends for years and Major North gave Cody a cordial welcome.

On this occasion Cody suggested to Major North that since the work of scouting was soon coming to an end, he ought to go into some business that was steady and safe. After a long talk, Cody finally said:

Let us go into the cattle business together. Everybody who is raising stock now is making money.

All right, I'll do it, replied the major and they talked over plans and came to a business understanding. It was agreed that Buffalo Bill and the North brothers, Frank, James E. and Luther, should form a partnership under the firm name of Cody and North, and that the Norths should have the management of the ranch, thus giving Buffalo Bill an opportunity to continue his profitable theatrical career.

In accordance with this decision Major North now proceeded with an outfit of men, horses and wagons, to select a ranch, and to improve the chosen site for occupancy. In those days in western and northern Nebraska, as in other parts of the west, there were vast unoccupied plains which afforded immense grazing ranges. These lands the cattlemen took possession of. Their only title was that of occupancy, yet the cattlemen had the right to purchase land if they pleased.

Major North located his ranch on the Dismal river in western Nebraska and remained there for a time, superintending the erection of the necessary buildings, which at first consisted of a log ranch house and a sod stable. He then went to Ogallala, on the Union Pacific railroad, to await the arrival of the cattle-drive from Texas. Here he was joined by his partners, his two brothers and Cody. At Ogallala, Major North purchased about fifteen hundred head of cattle and then branded them and drove them up to the Dismal river, where they were to be held. The ranch was located on the headwaters of the Dismal, about fifty miles north of the Union Pacific railroad and sixty-five miles northwest of North Platte station, the range being about twenty miles wide and thirty miles long. The ranch-house was strongly constructed of hewn cedar logs and was eighteen feet wide and thirty-six feet long. It was divided into two rooms, one being the kitchen and the other the living and sleeping room. It was located in a beautiful situation-a wide valley in the sand-hills about two miles long and a mile wide. In this valley there was a lake, half a mile long and a quarter of a mile wide, fed by clear spring water. The lake emptied into another lake half a mile distant, considerably larger. The valley was hay land, upon which grew fine grass in abundance and which because it was so near to the ranch, was very convenient and very valuable.

The Sioux Indians, from the various bands of Spotted Tail, and Red Cloud, roamed over this country, which was their favorite hunting ground and although they were then peaceable and friendly, Major North had his log house constructed with a view to protection, for the Indians were not always to be trusted and occasionally a hostile band might come down upon him unawares. Besides, the Sioux disliked Major North for the part he had taken against them as the leader of their enemies the Pawnees, and he knew that they would soon learn of his establishing a ranch on the Dismal river.

He accordingly had his men furnished with long range guns and other arms and a good supply of ammunition was stored in the house. Port-holes were made through the log walls on every side, so that the little fortress commanded the field in all directions. The corral and stable being located nearby were thus easily protected. The situation of the fortress was such that during the daytime Indians could not come within three-quarters of a mile of it, from any point, without being discovered. With all these precautions Major North felt secure from Indian raids.

Frank North had been troubled with asthma for years and little by little, this malady grew worse. Often it was impossible for him to lie down to sleep and for long periods he was obliged to sit up almost constantly. His uncertain naps in a chair were frequently interrupted by fits of coughing and gasping. As these distressing attacks came more frequently and also lasted longer, he was less at the ranch and spent more time at home or elsewhere in search of health. Finally it came about that the management of the ranch and of the cattle was carried on entirely by Luther North, who planned the work and looked after the range riding, the condition of the cattle, the round-up and the beef shipments.

For about five years the Norths conducted the cattle ranch here with great success and the story of what they did and what they saw there would be of real interest to many people, who know only by vague rumor of what life on the cattle range really was. Luther North, who is a keen observer, was constantly in the saddle out-of-doors and witnessed a multitude of interesting incidents and acts in connection with wild animals and birds and wild cattle which ought to be recorded.

Finally, in 1882, when more and more cattle were being constantly thrown on the range, when homesteaders were taking up land here and there, and the over-crowded grazing was growing constantly poorer, the Norths decided that for them free range on the Platte was at an end. They sold their cattle to a neighboring ranchman and finally retired from the frontier.

BIG BYTE BOOKS is your source for great lost history!

Made in the USA
Monee, IL
07 November 2021